I0165475

*"Leaders can learn how to use the creative hidden aspects of decision making to come up with new solutions to old problems"*

~ Tom Mitchell, Ph.D.
Co-Author of "The Winning Spirit" with Joe Montana

*"Howl! is a fascinating read providing wonderful analogies of the wolf and its pack to leaders in companies. This is a must-read for anyone in business who possesses a strong desire to succeed,"*

~ Elinor Stutz
CEO, Smooth Sale, LLC
Author of "Nice Girls DO Get the Sale"

Copyright © 2010

All rights reserved. Printed in the United States of America. No part of this publication may be reproduced, stored in a retrieval system or transmitted in any form or by any means, electronic, mechanical, photocopying, recording or otherwise without the written permission of the publisher. General references to the book name and type or brief quotation in printed reviews are an exception.

Published by
ClearEdge, LLC
20930 N. Tatum Blvd.
Suite 110-111
Phoenix, AZ  85050

**www.YourClearEdge.com**
ISBN 978-0-9823646-1-1

# HOWL!

## How to
## *LEAD • LEVEL • LEVERAGE*
### any Pack

by Deborah M. Dubree

# IT'S TIME TO HOW... LLL

## LEAD

To initiate - To show the way - To set in motion

Go in front of or beside

True leaders must first be SELF-Aware

Authority—Appreciation—Authenticity.

With these compelling traits ...

followers choose to join with true Leaders.

## LEVEL

Prepare for the future, today!

Remove the need for hierarchy

Allow leaders to flourish within every position and rank

Candid communication, creativity,
adaptability and awareness.

This is not soft leadership, it is feeling leadership.

## LEVERAGE

The power to influence

Enhance what is already working.

Recognize and unleash unrealized potential.

**Become the Alpha Leader of Your Life ... HOWL!**

# In Gratitude to My Wolf

Strong, powerful, proud

Intuitive and wise

Opportunistic and realistic

Focused on what Is

Striving for what can be

Sees the future

Grows from the past

Loving, nurturing, playful

Social and Lone

Mysterious and Majestic

**The Ultimate Leader
You HOWL!**

*This book is dedicated to
my two beautiful children
**Kristine and Jason.***

*You are my deepest love
and my greatest joy.
I am so proud of you!*

*Thank you for being you . . .
and for always encouraging
me to be me!*

*Love & Hugs,
Mom*

# Acknowledgements

*My heartfelt gratitude goes out to these powerful, creative and knowledgeable women whose assistance and guidance made "HOWL!" possible.*

**Laine Cunningham**, Writer's Resource, for your amazing editing, your expert guidance and your invaluable input.

**Randy Peyser**, Author One Stop, for your vast and valuable resources, your encouragement and sharing your knowledge.

**Vickie Mullins**, Mullins Creative, for your expert guidance, extraordinary cover design and genuinely caring about me and the success of this book.

*I am sincerely grateful to all of you!*

# Table of Contents

INTRODUCTION ...............................................11

CHAPTER ONE : Face Your Fables ...................17

Myth-Making in the Human World
Aunt Martha Stole the Cookies
How Real is the Real World?
The Why Behind the Wisdom

CHAPTER TWO : Find Your Real Place in the Pack.....37

Speak Your Truth
A "Good" Façade
Barriers Become Traps
Who You Are Not
Transform the Tragedy

CHAPTER THREE : Choose Your Path .........................55

You've Gone Rogue
The Brain and the Mind
Life in Survival Mode
The Power of Choice

CHAPTER FOUR : Aim for the Peak..............................75

A Bigger Cage
Flatline
Flatlining on the Job
Change the Scenario
The Power of Being Fully Present

CHAPTER FIVE : Remember Your Instincts ..................95

Energy at Work
Start with Energy
Energy in Action
Your Body Says It All
Yip, Howl and Growl

CHAPTER SIX : Level Your Pack.....................................115
  Leaders Cultivate Their Packs
  Train for Success
  Monitor Growth
  Show Your Appreciation
  Beyond Words

CHAPTER SEVEN : Avoid the Porcupines .................135
  No Time to Waste
  Wolf Attitude
  Allocating Your Hierarchy
  Kill Excuses

CHAPTER EIGHT : Express Your Power.....................155
  The Myth of Fear
  Power is Not Force
  Leadership Is about Energy
  Lead by Example

CHAPTER NINE : Bond with Your Pack.....................173
  Play for Profit
  Workplace or a Working Family?
  Playing Well with Others

CHAPTER TEN : The Wolf's-Eye View..........................191
  Inspired by the Lone Wolf
  The Spirit of Entrepreneurial Leadership™
  Feeling Leadership
  The Creative Corporate Culture
  It Begins with You

CHAPTER ELEVEN : The Ultimate Wolf Way............209
  First-Generation Results
  Which Wolf Wins?

BE CONNECTED.............................................................219

ABOUT THE AUTHOR..................................................221

# *Introduction*

You have two minds. I don't mean you're *of* two minds, that you're undecided about something. As a CEO, an entrepreneur, a manager or the owner of a start-up, you're clearly capable of making decisions. Still, you literally have two minds. Each mind has its own specialty, its own set of skills. When linked together, your two minds become one powerful force. Yet most of us utilize only one of these minds. That's like owning a high-performance race car that you only drive in first gear.

Wolves, on the other hand, use both of their minds. A wolf's wisdom stems from its instinct, knowledge and experience. But if the alpha wolf never takes its pack out to hunt, all of that wisdom goes to waste. You never see a wolf sitting on its haunches telling stories about the good ol' days. The pack won't allow it. Without wisdom in action, the entire pack will starve.

A wolf is active. It implements its knowledge for its own benefit and for the benefit of the pack. Leaders must do the same. They must turn their subconscious instincts, knowledge and experience into conscious actions that benefit themselves, their employees and their companies. A leader who doesn't will starve the company of success, enthusiasm and revenue.

That's not to say that wolves are always in high gear. They are, however, just like that race car—always ready to roar into life, always able to shift into whatever gear is needed at the time. Wolves achieve this through a state of restful alertness. They constantly assess their environment, the passage of time and the changing needs of their pack. They maintain their territorial boundaries and are ready to pounce on problems and opportunities.

Powerful, successful packs are created when leaders use both of their minds. The first mind is one with which humans are very familiar, the conscious mind. It's the one taught in business schools and any number of business books. The conscious mind is linear. It applies logic, information and experience to create plans and formulate structure. Because it is the seat of free will, because it's the method through which you make choices, it's the place of greatest power.

But the conscious mind isn't the entire picture. The other mind, the subconscious, works with feelings. It's the hidden aspect of decision making and leadership that often is either pushed aside or ignored. Yet it impacts every decision; every thought brings up feelings that impact your decisions and your actions whether you're aware of them or not. It is always at work. When you become aware of the process, you become the  Alpha Leader of your minds.

Take, for example, the stock market. Whenever stocks plunge, the subconscious hogs the spotlight. Financial planners and market analysts repeatedly tell investors to "resist panic." Panic stems from emotions. A panicked sell-off means not only a loss at the time of sale but also the loss of future revenue after the stock recovers. Yes, decisions can be made to ameliorate the situation. However, when respected analysts start talking about feelings, it's clear they understand that the subconscious mind can create chaos in a logic-based industry.

Your company is the same. Whether you are in sales or you head up a corporation or a financial department, your greatest asset is a collection of organisms that function through feelings: your employees. You yourself are a thinking *and* feeling person. Every employee in your company also has two minds, and their actions are impacted by their own unique feelings. We must be aware of our feelings, of our past experiences and lessons—whether our perceptions were accurate or not—that have been programmed into our subconscious and that affect every decision made by our conscious minds.

The stock market provides a real-world example of how the subconscious can sabotage logic. Yet our subconscious minds also offer qualities that, when applied in an appropriate way, yield tremendous benefits. One of a wolf's most powerful abilities stems from working without judgment, from knowledge that has not been tainted by emotions. The wolf is unattached to the outcome and performs courageous acts to achieve its goals. Similarly, the Alpha Leader of the mind gains the courage to make good choices, implement strong actions and imagine the opportunities beyond any crisis.

The creativity, imagination and lack of attachment you need to unleash your true potential can be taught—not at a university or by a traditional business book but through awareness, choices and training. Once you've freed the best aspects of your subconscious mind, your conscious mind can create the step-by-step plan that will achieve results. The wolf does the same by applying its best wisdom when it adapts to new circumstances.

Suddenly both minds work in tandem. You've found the highest gear, the point of greatest power. When you lead with your integrated mind, you inspire everyone around you—peers, employees, clients and even individuals in your personal relationships—to utilize both their minds. You set the example for how to release limiting thoughts and bring creativity and imagination into play. Their conscious decisions are therefore true . . . not only to their own version of the truth, which might be based on negative experiences, but to the truth of your shared values. You spark the internal combustion that ignites power in your company and your entire world.

My own wolf wisdom developed during my journey to financial and corporate success. Some years ago, I landed my first big job. A receptionist position might not sound like much, but I worked hard to improve every aspect of my life—to be a better employee, mother, creative thinker, friend and, later, boss. Along the way, I discovered shortcuts to peak performance. Eventually I became the owner of a $20 million construction company.

The tools I developed to create this kind of success helped me feel alive. They changed every aspect of my life, bringing power and purpose to everything I did. And since I learned how to live free from my past, free from previous events and the feelings they produced, I was able to look forward to my future without those limiting attachments. By operating without fears and doubts, I am able to make choices in the present that lead to my best future. This upward spiral has generated the success I enjoy today.

What worked for me also works for others. My employees were offered the same tools and generated the same results. My business pack worked together for the benefit of the company, and for the benefit of our clients and every other employee. I couldn't possibly keep quiet about these tools, so I stepped away from my CEO position to coach other leaders.

For nearly thirty years I've shared this wisdom. I've helped individuals from all walks of life create stronger interpersonal and intrapersonal relationships, which has freed their internal power so it can flow out to everyone and everything around them. By utilizing the conscious and subconscious minds, through awareness of both feeling and logic, my clients function at their own peak performance.

This book will teach you the same lessons. You'll strip away those false beliefs, negative patterns and lies that stop you from achieving more. You'll step into your personal power and accomplish what you and others have thought to be impossible. By instinctually living your ultimate success, you'll free others to do the same. It all starts with you.

I've included "cheat sheets" based on the material covered in each chapter. They condense the most important lessons you've learned along the way. Refer to them when situations arise. You'll immediately know how to be the Alpha Leader of your minds and how to help others become the same. Remember, too, that these cheat sheets are a physical representation of what's going on inside your subconscious—the imprinting of new stories, the expansion of your database with new information.

These sheets will act both as a review and as reminders for what to take with you as you move forward. Every time you look over these pages, you strengthen the neural networks that have replaced the obsolete patterns. Your new pathways become more efficient than ever. You might choose now and again to reread entire chapters; you might also copy certain cheat sheets and post them in your office or tape them to the sun visor in your car.

You might even make notes on the copies. Go ahead! It's all your choice. Write your own keywords or draw pictures that will trigger your subconscious automatic patterns, the ones you've chosen to remind you of your power and genius. And, when you discover ways that the cheat sheets are helping you to make decisions differently, please let me know! I look forward to hearing of your growth.

You'll also find another section towards the end of the book: a set of exercises, all geared toward taking you beyond the pinnacles you've already achieved. You'll learn the ultimate wolf way.

So, be an opportunist and follow the flight of a crow to a carcass. Create clever plans that utilize every pack member's specific skills. Approach your prey silently and with intense focus. Utilize all of your skills, senses and power by utilizing both your minds. When the hunt fails, shake off the pain, learn from the mistakes and try again. And when you succeed, celebrate with the pack. **Howl!**

# CHAPTER ONE

# Face Your Fables

One day a lamb went down to the creek to quench her thirst. As she approached the water, she didn't see a wolf that was standing at a bend further upstream. But the wolf spotted her right away.

"Hey, there!" the wolf called. "You're muddying up the water with your hooves."

Hunkering low, he stalked toward the lamb. She knew she could never outrun the large predator and began to tremble. Her only hope was in trying to reason with the creature.

"I … I didn't muddy your part of the creek," she said. "The water is flowing down from where you are. I couldn't possibly have done that!"

The wolf growled and continued moving closer. "That doesn't matter. I'm actually angry because I heard you were saying bad things about me to all of your friends. You must be punished for that."

"What? I never! Who told you that?"

"That's not important, either. I know you've told stories about me for years now. You're a liar!"

The lamb began backing up. The wolf's fangs were very large and glistened in the sunlight.

"That can't be right," the lamb said. "I'm not even a year old yet! Whatever you heard came from someone else. I wasn't even born when you first heard those stories! Please—"

"Well, maybe your father spread that gossip," the wolf snarled. "Or maybe it was your grandfather. It all comes down to the same thing in the end!"

With that, he pounced. He savaged that poor lamb and gobbled up every piece. When he was done, he laughed. Fear was the greatest appetizer of them all.

**Myth-Making in the Human World**

The story of the wolf and the lamb tells us one thing: wolves are evil. More than just predators, they actively work to instill fear in their prey. They're also deceitful. When the lamb protested, the wolf denied what it knew to be true. When faced with irrefutable facts—the lamb hadn't been born when the rumors began—the wolf refused to acknowledge its own lie.

This story, and thousands of others that play off the supposed evil nature of wolves, is a stereotype. Stereotypes are fables humans have created based on internal misperceptions of external appearances, on misinformation and on ignorance of others' motives. We express our stereotypes externally and apply them to individuals who are "outside" our specific group or who we consider to be different from us. The wolf prowling your hallways, then, might actually be a highly efficient employee prowling for every opportunity to make the company better.

The only way to separate stereotypes from reality is to understand how our fables are created. False assumptions are damaging precisely because people don't understand how or why they appear in the first place. The reason no one automatically stops myths from clouding their judgment is because stereotypes spring from the subconscious.

Our past experiences, our memories and even our current experiences are all stored in the organic database of our brains. This collection of information is unique to each person. The subconscious stores a memory as a picture complete with emotions attached. When an event in the present triggers a memory, the associations emerge literally as the subconscious recorded them: no judgment is applied, the feelings and perceptions come out just as they went in—like events recorded by a camcorder.

Here's the kicker: *what it records might not be true.* In the simplest of terms, you are likely basing many of your decisions in business and in your personal life on stories that might not be true … and you're not even aware that you're doing it.

Now, there is a reason for this automatic response. Way back when we lived in a dangerous environment, we needed to react without thinking. We needed to know that lightning might kill us or a bear might eat us. Reacting quickly, without making an informed judgment about whether *this* storm or *this* bear was dangerous, helped us survive.

Unfortunately, we also needed to know whether other humans might be hostile. The same automatic processing was applied to how a person looked. Someone carrying a weapon was clearly a potential threat. Even the clothes or body paint worn by members of different tribes was enough to alert us to danger.

At their core, these signals were processed as "other." A different tribe or a different species might mean us harm. As we moved into new territories, the unknown environment had plenty of hidden danger for us newcomers. Being alert to danger signals meant we could fight, flee or approach with caution. Even within our own tribes, signs of illness could trigger avoidance by other members.

What began as a survival instinct way back then leads to lack of understanding today. Lack of understanding leads to an inability to take appropriate action. The person viewed through the lens of a stereotype is judged incorrectly. The individuals applying the stereotype can't recognize that person's talents. Our myths—whether they are held individually or by a group—blind us to opportunities.

To achieve genuine, beneficial interaction, stereotypes must be uprooted from the subconscious mind. Only then can we determine an individual's real intention, motives and abilities. Only then can we utilize each individual for optimal performance.

**Aunt Martha Stole the Cookies**

Let's say you walk into a business meeting where you will close a million-dollar deal. When you shake hands with the vice president of the other company, something about the VP's personality reminds you of your Aunt Martha. Your conscious mind doesn't register the resemblance, but your subconscious has instantly made the connection.

Years ago at a family picnic, you saw Aunt Martha take two brownies off a tray and put them in her purse. She might have been taking them home to your uncle who couldn't attend the picnic. She might have been about to take a walk with your pesky nephew and wanting to keep him distracted. You don't know her real motive for taking the brownies, yet your subconscious mind recorded the myth: *Aunt Martha steals.*

Fast-forward to your meeting with the VP. You have a funny feeling you can't trust this woman. You question her and ask to see the records again, even though they've already been reviewed and approved by your chief financial officer. Not surprisingly, the meeting doesn't go as well as expected. Without realizing it, you made a million-dollar decision based on a myth about this VP instead of on her own merit.

Our perceptions of people, things, events or places can set up a database of information that bears consequences years later. Our minds constantly compare today's information to what's already been installed in the subconscious. In an attempt to figure out what to do, think, feel or believe, stories from the past bubble up.

In this example, neither side won. Both parties had to spend more time in the meeting because you asked to review the records again. Instead of focusing on the final details, both sides had to rehash what had already been settled. And trust me … the VP and the other representatives picked up on your sudden suspicion. With all of that raging inside, you have to ask: *Who's really the boss of you?*

## How Real Is the Real World?

Personality traits and mannerisms can trigger our subconscious in subtle ways. As much as we like to deny it, physical appearances can also trigger the same automatic responses. It's our most primal response and is difficult to override. During my own career, I experienced this type of automatic programming firsthand.

I once owned an International Race of Champions (IROC) Chevy Camaro. Fire-engine red, dual exhaust, side skirts, a high-performance 5.7-liter engine and chrome wheels with oversized racing tires ... clearly a force to be reckoned with. The license plate read XLR8ER (Accelerator). Enough said.

I'd always wanted to race cars and took control of a six-hundred-horsepower vehicle at the Richard Petty School of Driving. At the Bondurant School of Driving, I'd been a passenger as a race car driver careened into corners at ninety miles an hour. The IROC was a must-have! At the time, I was a controller in a construction company. I always wore professional attire and high heels. My makeup and hair were always impeccable, and I enjoyed every bit of my life. Especially the commute!

One day a company foreman asked, "Who owns that racy, badass IROC?"

Everyone in earshot thought I was kidding when I said it was mine. So I opened my desk drawer and pushed the alarm on my key ring. Jaws hit the floor when that racy, badass car began beeping.

Those people couldn't match up two very different stereotypical images that lived in their databases. I looked, acted and spoke like a professional ... a professional *woman*, no less. *And* I drove that red muscle car? Their internal computers came close to crashing. Their databases had always functioned just fine, regurgitating flat characters and old facts to help them understand new situations. This new situation couldn't be explained by anything they'd experienced before.

This meant, of course, that their databases probably had been giving them incorrect information about a lot of things. The guidance their conscious minds took from that faulty flow generated plans and actions that couldn't possibly achieve optimal success. When faced with the truth—that

I was powerful *and* fun—their databases, and their minds, were forced to expand.

Although the IROC might not have had a huge impact, other stereotypes can be extraordinarily detrimental. This lesson hit hard when I was diagnosed with Bell's palsy. When a cranial nerve suffers trauma, the facial muscles weaken. My right eyelid wouldn't shut so I wore a patch over that eye. My right cheek and part of my mouth drooped so much they appeared deformed. Smiling and talking and expressing my emotions could only be done with the left side of my face. To drink or eat, I had to hold the right side of my mouth shut so things wouldn't fall out.

It was quite a change. On top of that challenge, the palsy struck close to the holidays. I went to an upscale mall to do my usual gift shopping. Beautiful lights hung everywhere. The holiday music was barely audible over the voices of happy shoppers.

As I walked through the main corridor, strange things began to happen. People stared. Others caught a glimpse and then looked away. Others pointed. Children who were behaving perfectly suddenly had their hands snatched up by worried mothers who steered a wide berth around this unusual woman.

Well. I hadn't thought I looked *that* bad! Undaunted, I strolled into the first store for a sweater my mother had picked out of a sale ad. I rifled through a couple of racks without finding the right one. Finally I spotted a clerk.

"Excuse me," I said warmly. "Can you tell me where I can find these sweaters?" I showed her the news clipping. The moment she saw my face, her demeanor changed. She was clearly uncomfortable. When she spoke, her voice was so loud it shook the clothes right off the racks.

"They're on the upper level," she hollered. "I can take you there if you'd like."

"Thank you, that won't be necessary. I appreciate your help!" I gave her half a grin as I walked away. Half was all my face would allow.

I knew her intentions had been kind. It still hurt. She saw only my deformed face. She assumed I must be deaf and unable to find my way to the display. According to her database, I didn't look like someone capable of normal activities. Many shoppers made their own judgments. I looked different, therefore I was different. And since I was different, I must have been some kind of threat. At the very least, I wasn't someone with whom they wanted to associate.

The important thing was not how I looked but who I was. That got lost in the assumptions, the false facts, the automatic programming that leapt out of their subconscious minds. The stereotypes led to personal and professional consequences. Mothers felt threatened and passed along unspoken false messages to their children. Stores lost sales because their clerks were uncomfortable helping me. And, of course, I felt ostracized by a simple, temporary medical condition that was dangerous only to my own self-esteem.

As managers and leaders, it's important we recognize that people are our greatest resource. Once we eliminate the judgment of past experiences and outward appearances, we see everyone as people. Now, I'm not suggesting we do away with titles, hold hands and sing "We are the World." I am suggesting we address the business environment in an "eye-to-eye" approach.

If our view is "I to I" muddled with personal baggage, we can miss out on great ideas, creative planning and purposeful discussions. We also miss out on simply being connected to other people. When our view of someone is eye-to-eye, based in the reality of here and now, we can see the true worth of the other human being. We see their views and our own. We listen to all ideas instead of defending ours.

People are interesting. When you break down stereotypes, you discover who each pack member truly is and what each has to offer.

## The Why Behind the Wisdom

Your brain runs a thousand times faster than the fastest supercomputer in the world. No power shortage there. Your brain is always on; yes, even when you're sleeping or daydreaming. There are 60 trillion synapses in your cerebral cortex. These synapses form neural networks, pathways your brain has constructed to carry certain thoughts, memories, skills or information. Because these neural networks are interconnected, you have the ability to build complex ideas, memories and emotions.

Every time you have a thought, whether real or imagined, these neural networks fire. When the electrical currents spark, the brain produces a chemical or group of chemicals that generates a corresponding emotion. The chemicals are sent out to different parts of your body, and you feel a specific corresponding emotion. Your brain chemistry and physiology are wired together. The brain constantly sends out chemical impulses/feelings so you constantly *respond* to those feelings. Thoughts produce chemicals, which produce emotions, which produce body sensations; and then new thoughts emerge and the cycle begins again. It all happens in nanoseconds.

Whether you like it, deny it or ignore it, you constantly feel your emotions. This is precisely why stereotypes are so destructive. They reside in your subconscious and are

# Brain - Body Feedback Loop

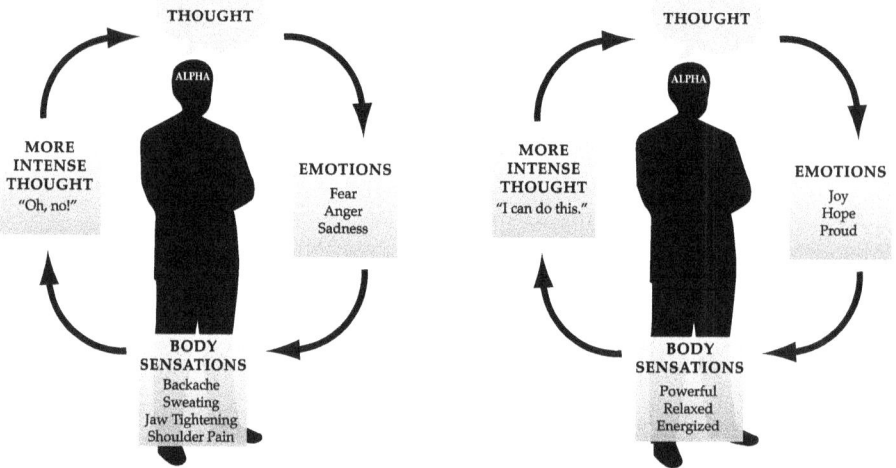

| THOUGHT | | THOUGHT | |
|---|---|---|---|
| **ALPHA** | | **ALPHA** | |
| **MORE INTENSE THOUGHT** "Oh, no!" | **EMOTIONS** Fear Anger Sadness | **MORE INTENSE THOUGHT** "I can do this." | **EMOTIONS** Joy Hope Proud |
| **BODY SENSATIONS** Backache Sweating Jaw Tightening Shoulder Pain | | **BODY SENSATIONS** Powerful Relaxed Energized | |

When we have a thought, our brain compares it to a *"like experience"* in our database. In a nanosecond our brain produces chemicals - which produce emotions and body sensations - which match our *experience* of the memory. The problem - this is automatic and unconscious. Our thoughts, emotions and body sensations intensify (good or bad) as we begin to focus on the effect, rather than their cause. It is up to the **Alpha of our Mind** to remain fully aware of these signals and shift the cause (thought), when necessary.

processed through emotional channels. Since they reside in your subconscious mind, you aren't aware of them consciously. Yet their effect interferes with your plans and actions.

*Every* thought you have is generated by interconnected neural networks. *Every* action you perform is based on prior experiences, assumptions and old information. You feel it in your body ... a tightness in your chest as you work with a new company, perhaps, or a thrill in your belly when you finally close that big contract. This continuous loop provides feedback to your body and brain, sending tension or joy around the track to emphasize and more-deeply implant the stereotype associated with each experience.

Remember that your subconscious mind processes information literally, not logically. Things don't *have* to make sense to be stored in that mind—it stores your *perception* of what you heard, saw or experienced. Since you were likely in a heightened state of emotion when you took in the comments or event, it's all implanted at the subconscious level. You created a myth, a story, which is played out again and again. You're unaware of it, yet the consequences remain yours.

Your logic, then, better be based on sound, accurate information. If it isn't, you and the recipient of the stereotypes will suffer.

## WOLF WAY #1: Exterminate Stereotypes

Wolves don't know how to worry. Wolves eat, drink, reproduce. They have emotions but they don't lament about the past. By staying in the present, and by dealing with the truth of their world, they can be productive and happy. Your goal is to view yourself and others without the lens of stereotypes.

Don't assume you know wolves are evil before you really study them. Don't project attributes like cunning, bloodthirsty and devious as part of an old story that was programmed automatically. Don't let what someone's father or grandfather said change how you view today's lamb!

To make that fundamental shift, you have to consciously understand how the subconscious works. What lies in that mind is registered as pictures, images that have been recorded through your five senses. There are no words floating around in there, only short films and stills you've collected from your life's Kodak moments. Pictures are the language of the subconscious.

To change our subconscious beliefs, we must use our conscious minds. We must choose to visualize not how things might have been but how things truly are. We must select one old belief and imagine something different. If you simply remove an existing thought, a void is left in its place. And like any smart predator moving into an abandoned territory, something will take its place.

If you allow the void to exist, the subconscious mind will fill it with something else. And because the subconscious also knows what used to be there, it will probably fill the void with something similar. You'll be no better off than you were with the original program. The image will be different, but the emotions and the perception attached to that image will be the same.

The conscious mind, then, has a double duty: to direct your subconscious mind to eliminate the old and to replace it with something new. That's the only way to eradicate the stereotype forever. You must prevent the old automatic program from coming back by giving the subconscious mind a powerful new specific experience to focus on—an experience of your new desired results. Since you choose what to place in the void, the process is extraordinarily powerful.

Suppose I want to use my mind to change a habit such as smoking. I access my subconscious mind by removing the distractions of the outer world and by focusing inward. Then I use pictures and feelings. I wouldn't imagine myself not smoking; instead, I would imagine what I feel like as I breathe clean air while hiking or taking my dog for a walk. I'd experience myself feeling this new energy. I'd put out a cigarette, saying no to it, because in my mind I feel so good without it. I use my imagination to create pictures and fully engage my emotions as if my new accomplishment had already occurred.

When you pinpoint your detrimental subconscious programs, you have the power to change them. By changing your thoughts and rewriting an old story as a truthful one, you no longer give your power away. Instead you take it back. You are awake, aware and amazed. You enjoy your peers, coworkers, friends and family. You gain courage and trust in yourself. Your confidence, skills and quality of life explode.

*Action step:* **Internal observation.** Recent studies have found that talent might not be "something you're born with." Individuals from sports figures to businesspeople who have achieved peak performance often showed no innate abilities even into their mid-twenties. Instead, talent is likely a function of practice, astute mentoring and internal observation.

Acute observation is the ability to watch yourself perform some task. The conscious mind is engaged in the activity itself while it also "takes notes." What works well, what needs to be improved, how you feel and how minute steps impact the outcome are all recorded by the acute observer. Clearly it requires a lot of focus.

To help you maintain this focus, use your imagination. Before engaging in the action you want to observe, visualize yourself floating up to thirty thousand feet. From your new vantage point, you can look down and watch yourself perform. As you perform your tasks, check in with this observer now and again. Make sure that you're consciously aware of everything you're doing, thinking and feeling. And have fun! Approach this like a virtual video game. Pay attention to how the other players make their moves so you can do better when it's your turn.

Suspend your judgment. Simply note when you experience what were once unconscious thoughts that have emotions attached to them. Your body might feel different due to that neurochemical feedback loop, indicating your subconscious has thrown something into the mix. You might find yourself distracted, working below maximum capacity, or facing some other difficulty that points to underlying complications.

Make a list throughout the day. The minute you become aware of a thought, emotion or behavior that's detrimental, you know you're not going to achieve the desired outcome. Are you slowing down a deal because the VP reminds you of your thieving Aunt Martha? Are you failing to utilize someone's talents because some petty external signal makes you think they aren't capable? Or are you allowing the stereotypes others apply to you change the way you operate?

Allow the acute observer to do the same in your personal life. Track anything that doesn't serve you that you nevertheless keep attracting. Study the relationships you have with people who annoy you. Think about the endless arguments with friends or family that never solve anything. Apply the same focus to these events, and note when your body feels different and when your thoughts become destructive.

You can't change anything until you're aware of your own stereotypes. Once you know what they are, you can work with the following steps to eliminate them.

*Action step:* **Dive deep.** Now that you have your list, you can look for the root causes. Trace back along those neural networks to the source. Locate the memory or prior event that is generating your present reaction. Search your database for the person, place or event that is bubbling up from your subconscious.

There are many ways to conduct this search. Look at what happened immediately before your feeling or thought arose. Who was in the room? Were you triggered by the spoken words or the expression on someone's face? When have you heard those words or seen that look before? Use your conscious mind to analyze the memory and the feelings associated with that memory. Figure out how your brain has organized the associations, the why of the recurring myth.

You might also check in with your body. Where did the neurochemicals end up? A tightness in the shoulders can mean you feel overburdened. A quick ache in the stomach might signal anxiety. Use your understanding of the brain-body feedback loop to locate the false information stored in your database.

Your subconscious mind can help with this search. Close your eyes. Take a deep breath and hold it for a minute. Then release it slowly. Go back to that lofty perch and imagine watching yourself again. When you reach the point where your feelings arose, stop the film. Ask your subconscious mind to provide an answer. Then, again without judgment, allow the hidden film to play in your mind's eye. You might have to wait a while before the film starts, but stay open. The Alpha Leader has given an order, and the subconscious mind will answer if you're patient.

*Action step:* **Write a new story.** Imagination is key. You're going to replace that old story with something new. You're going to fill the void so nothing detrimental ends up in its place. You're going to reinvent yourself, your thoughts and feelings to achieve peak performance in every aspect of your life.

This isn't done by "thinking it out." The conscious mind will relax, and your creative juices will begin to flow. Logical processes alone won't implement the change. If they could, they would have by now. You must engage your emotions to change the brain-body feedback loop forever. New inventions, enhanced prosperity and, yes, even happiness will follow.

The method is simple: Visualize new facts, a new way of being. Generate a new film, one that records the best of who you are and what you want. But this film is unlike any you've seen before. It includes sounds, smells and tactile experiences. You're going to touch, taste and smell everything you would in a real situation. The amazing thing about the subconscious is that it doesn't know the difference between an imagined event and one that takes place in the physical world. It therefore records your imaginary film as accurately, and as deeply, as your real experiences.

So visualize that untrustworthy VP. Imagine Aunt Martha standing beside her. Study them both closely. Realize that they dress differently, act differently and are two separate people. Nod to Aunt Martha as she leaves the room. Close the door firmly behind her and turn back to the VP. See her as if for the first time. Shake her hand, chat with her about how excited you are to close the deal and sit down to the real negotiation.

Take it further. Imagine every action occurring anew. Since you have no reason to suspect her, there's no reason to review the files. The meeting proceeds smoothly, and everyone is relaxed and enthusiastic. You sign the contract, and everyone leaves on time, excited about the opportunities that are now free of misplaced distrust.

If you have trouble during this visualization, repeat it. You've been carting around that old myth for years. Your subconscious might not want to let go of it right away. Each session that you repeat the visualization, it will become easier. That's because the old film is fading. The new film gains more color, more sensation, more "reality" with every retelling.

Soon your conscious mind won't have to order the film to run. The subconscious will cue it up automatically, generating a brain-body feedback loop that enhances all of your actions. Your two minds will work together for the benefit of yourself, your company and everyone you know.

## PAWS FOR REFLECTION

*Your underlying stories are often untrue,*
*yet their effect on you is powerful.*
*You are not your stories.*
*You are who you choose to be.*

## CHEAT SHEET

# Face Your Fables

- Stereotypes are fables humans create based on external appearances, misinformation and ignorance of others' motives.

- Stereotypes spring from the subconscious.

- The subconscious interprets literally what it has recorded. And what it records might not be true. It simply says "OK" to whatever it perceives to be true.

- Our minds constantly compare today's information to what's installed in our subconscious database to help us understand new situations.

- Your brain makes these connections so quickly that you aren't even aware they're happening. Brain chemicals flood into the body to generate a feedback loop that impacts your every thought, emotion and action.

- To change our subconscious beliefs, our conscious mind must make the choice to do so.

- If you simply remove an existing thought, the subconscious will fill it with whatever other pattern is most similar to the missing thought. The subconscious mind must imagine the new pattern with which to fill the void.

- Watch yourself from a thirty-thousand-foot level. This internal observer notes and records without judgment. Become aware of your stereotypes.

- Trace back through the neural networks to the originating memory or prior event. The way your body feels can help you pinpoint your triggers.

## CHEAT SHEET

- Write a new story. Create a new film that showcases you as the best of who you are. Experience what you want as if it already existed. Feel, smell, taste, hear and touch everything. Imagine this new film repeatedly until it's an ingrained response.

**Free tools at www.HowlLeadership.com**
*(Use VIP Code: ALPHA)*

# Find Your *Real* Place in the Pack

The pack has brought down a deer. It is a large, healthy buck with plenty of fat stored against the winter. The weather already is cold; and as the pack feeds, the first snow begins to fall. The wolves ignore it, just as they ignore the crows that have already gathered in the trees. The one thing they don't ignore is each other.

Feeding is a serious business, and there's an established order to who eats first. The highest-ranking pair, the alpha couple, is at the top of the chain. Since they're the only ones who reproduce, allowing them to eat their fill first makes sense for the entire pack. The health of the alphas ensures that the group will not die out.

The second highest also often take as much as they can eat. At the bottom is the omega wolf, the lowest-ranked adult member. The wolves constantly use body language and vocalizations to emphasize and maintain the pecking order. Around the carcass, their communication is in full swing.

Teeth are bared. Hackles rise. Tails stiffen as individuals

growl and tremble with coiled energy. Now and again, the discussion turns physical and snapping leads to nips and wrestling. A puff of fur floats on the wind; a muzzle bleeds from a nick. Eventually everyone settles in to finish the meal.

At the next carcass, at their next kill, the pack will do it all again.

## Speak Your Truth

Now, all of that snarling and snapping might appear chaotic to us humans. Actually, it's a very efficient method of communication. It reinforces pack hierarchy at one of the most critical moments, feeding time. Subordinate members test the boundaries while higher-ranking individuals reinforce their dominance. The growling and posturing serves a purpose, and the consequences for insubordination are immediate.

Wolves don't have facades. The alphas don't grumble and give way when a lesser wolf goes for the choice piece of meat. Instead, they claim what is rightfully theirs. It is their reward for their superior skills and knowledge. People, on the other hand, erect facades in every area of their lives. They shield their emotions, their innermost being, behind societal norms.

It starts at birth. Infants and children are like video cams. They collect their experiences as if what they're learning is the only way to live. As you mature, you might find that you don't like these ways of living, yet you haven't learned any other way to act. You cling to your old myths about the way things, and you, should be.

The father who has a lifelong career as a doctor has sons who become doctors. Since mom became a lawyer, her children are expected to become lawyers. They are pushed and prodded in certain directions, just like wolf pups are expected to take on different roles. These stories or expectations serve a purpose … a small-minded one. They fulfill some need or desire in other people. They do nothing to serve the big purpose in your life, the reason why you're on this planet. To be a peak performer and lead the pack, you must live from your true self.

We define ourselves early on. If someone is called a party guy because he gets wild every weekend, people who hear that also call him a party guy. The label sticks so well that he defines himself the same way. Even though he's much more diverse than the label implies, it becomes his story. When he enters the workforce, he slacks off at his job and in his personal life. He seeks out temporary, immediate pleasures and sacrifices nothing for his own future. It isn't long before he is left behind by his peers.

The worst part is that he's stuck there. He might not be consciously aware that he's striving to meet the expectations of others. At some point, he might become aware of what's happened, yet he doesn't do anything to change it. He might not know how to change, or he might be worried that he'll lose friends or allies at work. If he tries to change his place in the pack, he might end up worse off.

Perhaps you buy into how society has labeled you because you don't want to reveal too much of yourself. It's difficult to change—it's risky—and you might create chaos in your pack by even trying. Better to keep quiet, to never test the boundaries. Better to hum along in the status quo, changing masks to keep projecting all of the different facades people expect to see faster than you change clothes.

If you forget who you really are, though, if you buy into the false facades others have built for you, you're like the character Robert Downey Jr. played in the movie *Tropic Thunder*. He says, "I'm a dude playing a dude disguised as another dude." He's buried so deep in facades the original dude gets lost.

The same thing happens to you when you live someone else's truth. You might be and have everything that fits your definition of success, you might control millions of dollars and thousands of employees; but if you don't strip off the disguise and work with the real dude, you'll live a label that is only true for others.

## A "Good" Facade

Oh, how we love our bling. Our suits are tailored, and we drive luxury sedans, sports cars or whatever else is in vogue. We live in gated communities and accessorize our children with the latest electronics. We deserve the choice rewards for our skills and abilities, and we also want everyone else to know we're successful.

A client I coached through my consulting service was the same. She was a successful businesswoman with a husband and young children. She was clearly a leader in her field, an alpha enjoying the alpha lifestyle. Yet she wanted more out of life. She felt lost in daily repetition, and thought life had to be able to offer her more.

She was right. We worked together to locate the true source of her problem. She told me about a childhood event that had made her think she needed be perfect to gain her father's love. Her subconscious carried this memory into adulthood. No matter what she did, the feelings that impacted her every thought and action drove the same point home: *Be perfect if you want your husband to love you. Be perfect for your children. Be perfect for your peers.* Anxiety prevented her from enjoying her own life.

After our work, she recognized the truth. Her father had always loved her exactly as she was. She thought she needed to be a certain way, to maintain a certain facade, in order to be loved. But the need for perfection was self-imposed. She'd spent her entire life obsessing over the precise masks that would satisfy others. In the process, she'd entirely disregarded her true self, her own goals and any self-determined assessment of success.

This was an enormous breakthrough. Because she had located the initial experience, she had the power to change. I guided her through visualizing what her life would become now that she was relaxed and loved. The upward spiral she created through that powerful choice continues to create new prosperity and true happiness in her personal and professional life. Being perfect is no longer part of the equation.

She'd tried to project a certain facade for a "good" reason. Who wouldn't want to be seen as perfect? Who doesn't want to be loved? However, perfection is an unrealistic goal. The pursuit of any facade, even a "good" one, drains too much effort, time and energy. The worry, self-doubt and constant internal criticism distracts the mind from daily issues.

The impact is real for both professional and personal lives. Crisis cannot be effectively addressed, and the company never receives the benefit of the leader's full attention. Since their power and energy is drained to support the facades, goals fail to be achieved. When they are met, anxiety, fear and lack of real fulfillment make the victory ring hollow. The wolf's heart longs for more.

## Barriers Become Traps

Facades often are built for protection. They shield us from some pain, from again suffering the emotions or strife created by situations in our past. They also become barriers that prevent us from achieving peak performance and ultimate success. They lock out true achievement and keep us locked in.

When I was twelve, I experienced a painful tragedy that impacted much of my adult life: A few days before Christmas of 1964, I was baking cookies. The smell filled the house with sweetness. As I tasted the warm chocolate oozing around the edge of the pan, my best friend told me about a boy she liked at school. We laughed, told stories and sang carols.

The music was so loud I almost didn't hear the doorbell. I rushed to see who had stopped by. This was Lockport, a small town outside of Chicago, and everybody knew everybody. Since it was so close to Christmas, I thought it might be carolers. Standing in the darkness were my minister and a man dressed in a pinstriped suit.

"Are your mom and dad home?" the minister asked.

"They're over at the Blue Willow restaurant for a Christmas party," I said.

I slowly closed the door. Suddenly I felt cold. Something wasn't right. Moments later, I heard the garage door open. I crossed through the kitchen to the door into the garage. I flung it open, eager to share the magnificent cookies with my parents.

A line of four solemn people trooped in. Our minister and the well-dressed man were part of the procession. Mom and dad were crying. I was confused; what was happening?

"Stevie's dead!" mom screamed. "Stevie's dead!"

*I don't understand.*

Dad said my brother Steve lost control of his car. It hit a boulder and he died.

*This doesn't make sense*, I thought. *How can that be? What do you mean, he's dead?* **He's sixteen years old!** *Old people die, people*

*I don't know die—not sixteen-year-olds! Not my brother! What boulder? There are no boulders on the streets of Lockport.*

My head pounded, my heart ached and tears streamed down my cheeks. I'd never felt like this before. What did this mean? What was I supposed to do? I watched my parents as if I were inside a bubble. I felt their anguish. I heard their long, mournful cries. Dad tried to comfort my mom, who was out of control with grief, while waves of gut-wrenching pain wracked his body.

Eventually I heard the whole story. My brother and a friend had been driving into the country to see where a girl they knew lived. There was only one boulder along the entire two-lane road. For some unknown reason, the car swerved and hit it.

As friends and relatives surrounded our family, I received lots of attention. Certain people seemed to be in charge of making sure I was all right and that I was kept busy. As I answered stupid questions and played games I didn't want to play, my dad started screaming.

"Open the goddamn door or I'll break it down!" he shouted.

Dad never raised his voice. Something was wrong … very, very wrong. He was beating on the bathroom door. *Oh, my God*, I thought. *Mom has locked herself in the bathroom and he's afraid she's going to kill herself!*

An arm scooped me up from behind. I was whisked away to once again be protected and kept busy.

For almost twenty years, I lived out the survival stories I'd written, purely subconsciously, the days and weeks after Steve's death. Since losing control of his car resulted in his death, I learned to control my life, my feelings, my circumstances and my world. I planned everything to the hilt. Good for a work environment, not so much fun on a vacation. To continuously feel I had to stay in control was hard to live with … both for myself and my relationships.

Because I had been having fun and laughing just before I heard the horrible news, my new programming/survival story only allowed me to enjoy "controlled fun." Otherwise, something bad might follow. My life lacked real spontaneity, and I could never truly enjoy any of my achievements—it was too dangerous.

I had been kept busy so I wouldn't have to feel. Instead, I stayed inside that bubble, inside numbness. I graduated from high school, powered through cosmetology school, took my state boards, got my first real job, got married and had my first child all before I turned nineteen. Then I became an entrepreneur. I moved to Phoenix and landed a job in construction. I worked fifty-five hours a week and built a world filled with facades that trumpeted success.

But nothing penetrated my inner world to create true fulfillment. I couldn't risk the pain of letting anything in.

**Who You Are Not**

Let's get down to two of the most important questions you could ever ask: "Who am I, really?" and "What identity have I taken on that's not really me?"

There's the physical you, the intellectual you and the emotional you. The physical you can be seen, described, tested, prodded and probed. Others can sense the intellectual you by reading your résumé, checking out your accomplishments, listening to you speak, peeking into your office, even looking at your financial portfolio. But the emotional you is where all of the good stuff happens. It's where you experience life.

Your personal and professional excellence is governed by

the emotional you. The way your thoughts are processed through the subconscious with all of its embedded emotions makes it so. Your ability to make clear decisions will change when you stop the mental chatter that clouds your thoughts. Imagine the increased power, control and clarity you'll feel when you operate from your integrated mind rather than primarily from your subconscious.

You're not your job, your successes or your failures. You're not the words you speak or the amount of wealth you've accumulated. No matter how great your intellect, how amazing you look or how financially well-off you are, if your mind chatter is full of doubt, worry and fear, you can't enjoy all of your success. You must alter your inside so you can fully live the real dude on the outside.

Wolves don't add an emotional charge to their experience. They remember a lesson, but they don't turn dramatic. Humans, however, do. We internalize events and apply a false interpretation. The lesson often gets lost. You might say there's no place for emotions in your role as a professional businessperson/athlete/performer. Emotions make you weak; they hold you down. As the leader of yourself and others, you can't afford to show your emotions.

I hear you. I used to believe I had to keep my emotions in check—push 'em down and deny they even existed. The problem is, whether you deny them or not, they're still inside you. They create the facades that are meant to protect you. However, these same facades generate internal turmoil. They don't match up to your true desires and needs, yet your subconscious constantly returns to them more quickly than the rational mind can register.

Events in our lives take us through ups and downs. It's like a chart tracking the price of a stock—the chart records both peaks and valleys. Ideally, like the price of a successful stock, our emotional experiences show minor dips but overall indicate that lessons have been learned. Tragedy hurts like hell, but we recognize it, name it, and take something valuable from it. If we don't, the graph flatlines. There's no progress. No peaks. No joy of living.

## Transform the Tragedy

After my brother's death, I believed I had to stuff my feelings down so deeply they could never come back to hurt me again. What a different lesson I would have learned— and what a different life I would have led—if something different had been modeled. If I'd been encouraged to feel the pain and release it, I could have replaced it with gratitude for having had a brother for twelve years. It would have enhanced the value of my experience and allowed me to learn from it, rather than reinforcing the negative aspects.

In the decades during which I lived my false story, I couldn't possibly have enjoyed life. How different my life became after I identified the programming that had controlled me since childhood. I transformed the immense energy around Steve's death. I now feel a deep gratitude for the time we had together.

I still miss him and wish he were here, but the sabotaging stories and negative charge have been transformed. I can truthfully say I enjoy who I am. I have fun, and I freely express my deepest emotions. I give myself permission to explore and expand. I enjoy being an adventurer, traveler, speaker, author and coach. I continue to evolve.

My experiences have led me to dig deeply into how the human mind works and, more important, how to use the mind as it was meant to be used—for personal benefit and growth. My clients are amazed when they remember past incidents, identify their subconscious stories and break through barriers they've created. They learn they can be the boss of their thoughts and leaders in their lives.

You might not be ready to accept that your feelings impact your every thought, especially when you've already achieved major career success. Yet I see feelings impacting my clients over and over in my coaching profession. One client was a financial entrepreneur. He couldn't figure out why, despite being so successful, he experienced great trepidation when it came to leading his team.

His stories prevented him from enacting effective and efficient methods to accomplish his goals. While still in grade school, he'd been given the lead role in a play. During and after the performance he was ridiculed, people laughed at him and a loving family member became angry with him. All of these experiences became an unconscious story about how hurtful it is to be a leader.

By working with me to imagine a new story, he released the massive emotional energy the event had generated. With the experience now merely a memory and the emotional pain and embarrassment eliminated, he easily imagined his future as a confident, effective, successful business leader. His ability to lead, which he had masked, now flourishes.

Be like the wolf. Strip away all of those facades you think protect you but that actually trap the real you. Project who you truly are. Automatically lay claim to the choice piece as your due reward. Feel who you are, and own the power that enables you to perform at your peak. Live your true self in every area of your life for the greatest benefit of yourself and your pack.

## WOLF WAY #2: Strip Away the Facade

Your myths and stories have taken a lifetime to build. The process of eliminating them and fully becoming the Alpha Leader of your life offers a worthwhile reward. Taking responsibility for your thoughts and emotions comes first. Start by uncovering some of your own subconscious facades—the patterns that project the dude you are not to the world, the facades that trap you in dissatisfaction and anxiety.

*Action step:* **Feel your dissatisfaction.** In my own life, every time I achieved something, I was left wanting more. I celebrated, yes, but then I quickly returned to that state of striving, frustrated over what I thought was still out of reach. Those feelings had nothing to do with the incompleteness of the success and everything to do with my incomplete ability to celebrate.

To move into true success, I had to locate the real problem. I had to search back through my database to find the event that forced me to project a false dudette. The actions and plans clearly weren't the problem; everything in my linear world resulted in the precise goals I set. Only by identifying the feelings that bubbled up during current events could I search prior experiences for the same emotions.

Think about something that happened recently that left you dissatisfied. Maybe you were so anxious about presenting at a conference that you couldn't enjoy the moment. Even the praise you received afterward felt more like relief than anything resembling true joy.

Pinpoint the feeling that created the anxiety: fear of failure, thoughts that you might let your company down or sheer stage fright. Now search your database of past events for those same feelings. What previous experience made you feel like a failure or like you'd let someone down? It might be as simple as a poor grade on a college exam or as serious as a bankruptcy.

Once you've located one event, keep searching. Was that event symptomatic of other things that happened even earlier? Keep going until you locate the inaugurating event. Along the way, notice if you've allowed each new event to generate even more internal turmoil that strengthens those same emotions.

*Action step:* **Become aware of the facade.** Once you know what the feelings are and why they occur, you must determine how they impact your life. Fear of failure can prevent you from taking the risks necessary to grow your business to a phenomenal level. Not wanting to disappoint people can keep you locked into a staid pattern that squelches creative thinking. Anxiety over public performance can shake the confidence of your employees every time you move outside your circle of peers.

Once you've considered your career, look at your personal life. Your relationships with family and friends might suffer from the same lack of spontaneity and courage. Since the facade you present to them might be very different than the one you project at work, you might feel pressure when the two worlds mingle. Your confusion over which dude to be at the company picnic can be misinterpreted. Because you switch between facades, you come off as deliberately deceitful.

*Action step:* **Dismantle the facade.** No amount of chanting affirmations or deductive reasoning will help you change. Your conscious mind must allow the subconscious to release the emotions surrounding the original event.

One way is to sit with the original feelings. In my case, I had to revisit the days and weeks after Steve's death, the time in which I had been kept busy. I had to return to that original moment when I'd heard the news and to allow all the emotions of the moment to come back. Yes, it was painful; and yes, I had to be strong enough to grieve. But until I experienced the moment as I should have, I couldn't release the shock, pain and anguish created by that loss. I chose to relive it once and experience the truth of the moment rather than continue to give power to the facade that had plagued me.

Do the same. Find a quiet place where you can watch your own film again. Remember every detail of the scene: what you were wearing, the saturation of light in the room, the particular scent of the air. Allow the feelings to come up … finally … and simply be aware of them. Cry if you must; laugh when you feel like it. Be compassionate with yourself: the self you were, the one who took on too great a burden, the false facade that was meant to protect you. Then imagine what it's like now that you are free of the burden.

*Action step:* **For your own benefit, forgive those who hurt you.** Every human being has the potential for astonishing good. Rather than allowing negative thought patterns to rule your life, choose to feel compassion for the individuals who burdened you with false stories.

A healer once went to a prison and asked to see the files for individual convicts. As he paged through each file, he noticed the emotions that arose inside him. He healed those emotions in himself. Even though he never met the convicts, his compassion generated benefits for those individuals. He didn't forgive them for their acts but he did forgive *them*.

When we speak about forgiveness, we're talking about letting go of judgment and blame. You are not condoning their acts. You are taking your power back. You no longer allow resentment or blame to control you. You must tap into your own profound ability for good and offer forgiveness and heartfelt love for every individual involved in your past stories. And forgive yourself for having given away your power in the past.

When you achieve this level of ability, you are able to offer others your personal best. Everyone around you—from employees to family and friends—will benefit. Your achievements become exponential because they are based on a foundation of inner joy and compassion for your own true self.

*Action step:* **Go to the end result.** Now that you've eliminated those old feelings, replace them with something new. Visualize how you will feel with every new success. Engage all your senses. Feel yourself signing that contract and the strong handshake of congratulations. Hear praise being bestowed upon you. Taste the victory dinner, and see the vibrant colors of the world. Know that you deserve this greatest reward, that you are the alpha of your own domain. Be the true wolf inside.

## PAWS FOR REFLECTION

*When you are truly happy, fulfilled and enthusiastic,*

*you are your own true self.*

## CHEAT SHEET

# Find Your *Real* Place in the Pack

- Facades serve only the needs, desires and hopes of other people. They prevent you from showing who and what you really are.

- Even facades projected for a "good" reason—to achieve love, to obtain success—drain your time, effort and energy. The wolf longs for more.

- Facades built to protect you from some pain will always trap you. You'll never allow true happiness or fulfillment to penetrate the walls.

- You must alter your inside so you can fully live the real dude on the outside.

- Tragedy hurts, but don't flatline. Recognize the event, name it, shift it and take something valuable from your experience.

- Your feelings impact your every thought. Feel who you are and you'll own the power to perform at your peak.

- Thoughts produce chemicals, which produce emotions, which produce body sensations; and then new thoughts emerge and the cycle begins again. It all happens in nanoseconds.

- Your myths and stories have taken a lifetime to build. Eliminating them offers phenomenal rewards.

- Feel your dissatisfaction. Pinpoint the originating event, and understand how it impacts your current life. Release the shock, pain and anguish of whatever losses you've experienced in the past. The facade that burdens you will fall away.

## CHEAT SHEET

- Offer forgiveness to individuals who placed burdens on you, though you do not have to excuse their actions. And forgive yourself for having given away your power in the past.

- Visualize how you will feel with every new success. Replace the old stress and anxiety with relaxed confidence. You will be the alpha of your own domain.

**Free tools at www.HowlLeadership.com**
*(Use VIP Code: ALPHA)*

# Choose Your Path

Wolves only attack when they're hungry. Their true essence isn't negative or malicious or conniving. One night in the tundra of Denali National Park, Alaska, I spent hours watching a pack of wolves. When they spotted a group of rams and ewes, they looked for the weakest animal. They signaled to each other and made tail movements to communicate their positions as they set up the attack.

Sometimes, though, a wolf's natural behavior is corrupted. A rogue might slaughter livestock despite the fact that its habitat is healthy. Nationwide, only a hundred cattle, calves and sheep are killed every year by wolves. Their clear preference is for game animals—the cautious stalking, the explosive chase, the satisfying end.

When that natural preference is disrupted, chaos ensues. The wolf that prefers the easier targets presented by tame, sluggish livestock isn't operating at peak performance. His skills blunt. If ever he is forced back to his regular lifestyle, he's less able to survive. Then, when concerned humans get involved, the chaos spreads. Ranchers hunt any wolf on their properties, including packs that are happy to ignore cattle and sheep. The packs lose valuable members, move to a different territory, or die out completely.

The chaos spreads in ever-widening circles. Fewer predators means that a larger number of sick and aging deer, elk and moose survive longer. They have more contact with healthy members of their herds and infect others. Diseases spread from the wild populations back to the livestock, decimating herds and threatening the health of people when sick animals slip unnoticed into the food supplies.

All because a single rogue wolf didn't live the way nature intended.

### You've Gone Rogue

The human brain constantly records data, comparing the incoming information to the database of information it has already compiled. Because our memories are always tied to emotions, we analyze all experiences based on the emotions they generate. With every new experience, a storm of neural networks fire off thoughts, trigger memories and generate feelings.

The brain looks for similarities and connections to help sort out the new experience. Your brain is chock-full of memories, so everything in your present—and your plans for the future—is constantly being tied to the past. If that's appropriate, great! If not, your mind gets caught up in a chaotic pattern that creates confusion and prompts you to err in judgment.

Say you're reading this book when suddenly you feel the warmth of the sun shining through the window. You remember a sunny day when you enjoyed lunch in a restaurant with a friend. Then you smell someone's cigarette; you sadly remember the parent you lost to smoking. You recall the great times you had with that parent, and then your cell phone rings. You're jolted back to the present. This jumble started with your intention to read this book!

You were swept away by a stream of automatic, unconscious, routine, familiar, common, habitual thoughts. Think about it … it happens to all of us on a daily basis. A simple nudge unleashed a cascade of beliefs, memories and associations. Your mind jumped from one item to the next, feeling a surge of emotions along the way. This chaotic pattern temporarily took over. Your thoughts went rogue, leading you far from your chosen territory and preventing you from achieving peak performance.

Automatic patterns are often considered negative because they generate chaos. It's clear that the automatic patterns built in the past often are self-sabotaging. The patterns were created by someone else's needs, expectations, desires and thoughts—which you accepted. Since they weren't based on your needs, your values, your goals or desires, how could they possibly be healthy for *you*?

Instead, your mind can create a positive flow. You can choose to utilize automatic patterns that serve every aspect of your life. The subconscious can't be stopped from making connections; those neural networks are pure biology. Your conscious mind can perform a type of surgery, though. You can direct it to extract those chaotic patterns, to rewire the neural networks. Your every thought and action will then be based on real connections and supportive emotions.

To do this effectively, you must replace the chaotic pattern with a healthy one. Simply eliminating the old pattern leaves a void … and the subconscious mind doesn't like that. Its purpose is to help the conscious mind interpret new experiences quickly. A void in any part of the neural network means it can't function at its peak. Since the interactive survival mechanism was built into our brains long ago, you must work with the system, not against it.

Think of your subconscious as a child—a very powerful child but one who works on instinct rather than thought. Without guidance from the conscious mind, the subconscious will replace the old chaotic pattern with whatever is most similar to what's missing … and remember, that means a different chaotic pattern! The conscious mind is the adult who directs the child's activities. It chooses which pattern will be healthy and helpful and then instructs the subconscious to fill the void with that specific thing.

Now you are utilizing both your minds. You are adapting the most powerful component of the subconscious, the ability to make automatic, ingrained connections, in ways that support the conscious mind. Whenever you select a specific internal process, you do so for your own greatest good … and for the good of your pack. You create a new instinct, one based on your experience and wisdom, your knowledge and goals.

The more you train your mind to make these positive, useful connections, the more powerful your new patterns become. You'll function at your peak level because you've chosen the path best suited to your natural skills and abilities. You'll bypass the sluggish livestock and pursue the strong, swift prey. You'll avoid being sidetracked by rogue thoughts, because those chaotic automatic patterns have been reconditioned to positive, powerful ones.

## The Brain and the Mind

The brain and the mind are not the same thing. The brain is the organic gray matter encased in your skull. Different kinds of cells have built nerves and synapses. The neurons trigger cascades of chemicals that enter the bloodstream and flow out into your body. Your brain is the physical organ in which your minds reside.

Your mind—both of your minds—are the collection of experiences, memories and judgments created during your life. Since only you have experienced that exact sequence of days and events, your minds are utterly unique. Together, they constitute the intangible wisdom that works via the physical networks of the brain.

Thus emerge the automatic patterns. The physical pathways in the brain offer your thoughts certain roads. Some are superhighways to brilliant, capable management of every aspect of your life. Others are tangled and overgrown with negative emotions and memories that snare you in chaos. Because the physical brain is adaptable, because you have the flexibility to change the networks and clear out the overgrowth, your mind has the ability to create better roads to speed you on your way.

You are talented, intelligent and capable, yet one *minuscule* thought sends you into an emotional upheaval that seems to have no exit. The cascade has turned rogue. Your clear, calm, amazing mind has been poisoned with an isolated thought. It's like drinking a glass of water that contains a single drop of poison. Your genius suffers a painful, numbing death. You spin into a downward, uncontrollable spiral.

Your original thought probably dipped back to a deep-seated event from the past—a time when you first unconsciously took on the judgment of being "not good enough," for example. The originating thought might have triggered a new synaptic connection, a chaotic pattern, as your mind checked its database for similar thoughts and emotions. Jumping from one thought to the next added to your feeling of being out of control.

Wondering if your actions are good enough is the originating negative thought. While that might seem pretty harmless ... after all, we constantly have to assess our performance and that of others ... for your subconscious, it really means, "I hope *I'm* good enough." The negative thought is the trigger for the entire cascade that follows.

The subconscious responds the way it knows best, by finding memories associated with the same thought. Negative emotions rise up. Brain chemicals associated with fear, panic, anxiety and confusion are pumped out. The body responds with negative sensations such as perspiring, a pounding heart or a slumping posture. Because your mind gets feedback from the body, you take negative action. You yell, drop papers and scurry away to your office or the next meeting to avoid the situation.

Afterward, since you're human, you reflect on your reaction. Feeling bad about how you handled the situation leads to a new negative thought. That sets off another cascade of chaos. *I feel bad* leads to *I'll be fired* which leads to *How will I tell my spouse?* and finally to *I need rest.*

The entire scenario created or strengthened a negative neural network in the brain. It also created or strengthened ongoing problems—your body felt the negative emotions in a heightened way, the mind was overtaken by rogue thoughts and your less-than-stellar actions created more problems.

In business relationships—and any other type of relationship—these chaotic patterns kill your passion, push you out of sync with your purpose and steal your power. While your database of myths and stories can be the source of the triggers, so can elements in your environment. When the actions of your boss or peers don't match what they say, it creates confusion. When your morals and those of the company leaders aren't aligned, doubt arises. If you think you can't speak your mind, constant censoring creates anxiety. The effects cost you physically, mentally, emotionally and financially.

Since your thoughts, feelings, body sensations and actions are so closely interwoven, if even one of these elements falls out of alignment, others do as well. Stress follows. Pacing, sleepless nights, headaches, backaches, shoulder pain, an upset stomach, irritability, agitation, lethargy and absent-mindedness are all signs that something's wrong. Your subconscious is sending signals to your body to try to wake up your conscious mind. It's saying, "Listen up!"

## Life in Survival Mode

Jim is his company's new executive vice president. In fifteen minutes, he will make a crucial presentation to his key managers. Their understanding of Jim's plans and how next year's operations will be implemented rely on how well this presentation goes. It's his day to prove he's at his best. He must make a good impression.

Jim looks at his watch and smiles. He's confident and self-assured. He glances through his presentation a final time, knowing a lot of effort went into formulating the plan. Then he reflects on the company. Recently things have been tough; the team really needs a boost. His presentation *has* to get everyone on the same wavelength for everything to succeed.

His heart pounds a little faster. He scratches a few new ideas in the margins and reconsiders his conclusion. Suddenly he's burning up. He begins to pace, panicked about how to instill a clear edge into the presentation. Then he spots his image in the mirror. He's sweating so heavily his shirt has become damp.

He yells for his assistant to grab another shirt, and then he immediately feels bad for having yelled at her. If he screws up like that during the presentation, he might lose his job … or at the very least, the respect of his team. Without faith in his plan, the team won't implement everything properly and the entire initiative will fail. He's facing a year of failure, a year that will surely culminate in him being fired.

If that happens, how could he ever tell his wife? They haven't been able to spend much time together lately. They have a romantic vacation planned; can he really afford to be gone that long if the team isn't functioning properly? What will happen on the home front if he can't spend more time with his wife? Is he really going to have to make a choice?

Then reality shows up again. He's already late for the meeting. He screams at his assistant to help gather up his notes. As they scramble, he drops the papers, scoops them up and races down the hall. Hunched over with the burden of his thoughts and all of those neurochemicals, Jim bursts into the conference room. The presentation will fail because of one miniscule thought: *Is this good enough?*

Living with stress is like living in survival mode all of the time. You constantly look for and anticipate problems. When alerted by a thought, your fight-or-flight reaction kicks in. Your body prepares itself instantly. Your heart rate and blood pressure increase, pumping blood away from your brain and into your extremities so they can take action.

The body's response loops back to your brain. Your mind races, anticipating the next event to which it must react. Your thoughts are steeped in a high state of arousal as the new experience is compared to past events in your database. You lose the ability to think clearly.

The minute you allow your automatic patterns to go rogue, you lose your ability to reason. Your body and brain are ready for a fight. If a lion meanders into your office, you're ready to wrestle it to the floor. But when a lion doesn't show up, the blood and brain chemicals coursing through your body give you no edge. Instead, they leave your mind unprepared, snarled in the emotional overgrowth and unable to determine clear, appropriate action.

## The Power of Choice

All of this can be changed. Every individual has the power to break the old patterns. Choice is the key. You must choose to change, to do the work to locate those old stories that generate the feedback for failure. When you do, the same thought-emotion-neurochemical brain-body feedback loop allows your genius to function unfettered. The most powerful aspects of both of your minds work together to create your optimal success.

Many people aren't taught how to do the inner work of feeling and releasing emotions. Although we don't realize it, we actually do this spontaneously. When I was seven years old, I broke my right arm when I fell off a neighbor's porch. In addition to getting twenty-two stitches, the nerve in my arm had been pinched. Since I'm right-handed, the injury was quite a handicap.

The doctor said I might never regain the use of my right arm. Rather than allowing that diagnosis to stand unchallenged, my mother worked with me every day to bring movement back into the arm. It was painful, but she encouraged me constantly. Her mama wolf instincts sent me down a path to full recovery.

I responded to her determination and belief and actions in the moment. Because she modeled such a great scenario for me—that of choosing actions for my own greatest good—later in my life I was able to tap into this mama-wolf energy. When faced with the diagnosis, she could have set up an automatic pattern of helplessness, a spontaneous processing of negative emotions. Instead, she showed me the power of choice.

My friend Tony hadn't been so lucky. Whenever he planned to go out to dinner with someone, he'd start to choke. The panic response was much more serious than simply coughing. His throat felt as if it was closing up, and he'd gasp for breath. Sometimes it happened before he left home. Other times we'd be driving to the restaurant, when suddenly he'd pull over, fling open the car door and hang his head outside while trying desperately to breathe.

He visited a battery of doctors, and even ended up in the emergency room. The medical professionals found nothing wrong. There were no tumors or obstructions, no swelling or allergies. His only relief came from lying down right away to nap. Out of desperation and exasperation, Tony made an appointment at Mayo Clinic in Minnesota.

Three days of testing ensued. Nothing was physically wrong, and they could find no psychological problem. These famous, highly skilled doctors recommended he read a specific book. The narrative described how stress can generate a series of thoughts that create what feels like real symptoms of a major illness. Becoming stressed about the symptoms evokes even deeper and more pronounced negative thoughts. Thus the loop continues.

Fortunately, Tony paid attention. He uncovered a childhood memory of a time when a Halloween candy wrapper had lodged in his throat. He'd choked on it, and his subconscious believed he would die. Only sleeping, which blocked out all of the thoughts and feelings associated with this memory, alleviated the symptoms. The memory was triggered by his anticipation of a dinner out, a treat as pleasurable for the adult as Halloween candy should have been for the child. Once he knew what the problem was, he was able to short-circuit the brain-body feedback loop associated with that memory.

I don't want to imply that Jim or Tony or *you* are victims of chaotic patterns. I don't believe in victimhood, in suffering circumstances over which you have no control. The truth is that you simply need to become aware of the chaotic patterns. Then you can choose to change them.

Rather than being negative examples, these stories prove how amazingly powerful the mind and brain are. They can work for us or against us. The choice has always been and always will be yours. Round up those rogue thoughts. Remove them and replace them. Don't give them a place in the territory of your brain. Become the Alpha Leader of your minds. Use free will to set your focus on what you want. This is the power and the privilege of being human.

Automatic patterns can be extraordinarily beneficial. It's up to you to build ones anchored in truth that serve your purpose. Doing so will reinforce your purpose and power as an imaginative, effective leader. Every day, your challenge is to become more aware—that is, to consciously catch yourself at the beginning stages of a potentially chaotic pattern. Stop it, redirect it, laugh at it. Then you can form new, self-affirming patterns. No matter how rough things get, you'll have trained yourself to use these new instincts. You'll automatically achieve peak performance.

Just look at Michael Jordan. As any focused, high-performing athlete does, he constantly practiced the basics of basketball. The automatic patterns he built around the fundamentals of the game allowed him to be spectacular when three defenders were hanging all over him. It gave his subconscious mind the freedom to be creative and imaginative—his true genius showed up. He understood how important knowledge and skill were to his game. He utilized the power of his mind for his supreme benefit and that of his team.

### WOLF WAY #3 : Seize the Power of Change

At the first sign of a negative thought, Jim could have calmed down and reminded himself how prepared he was. He could have relied on his background and capabilities. He could have imagined how impressed his peers would be once they'd heard his plan. Any of these steps could have stopped the cascade of negative thoughts.

If he missed the initial thought, he could have checked in with his body. The increased heartbeat and the sweating were clear signals that his mind was working with chaotic, negative patterns. Then there were the environmental clues—yelling at his assistant, dropping his papers, and ending up late.

Once you recognize the need for this work, the process is really quite simple. Locate the harmful patterns. Transmute the emotions around those patterns and reprogram them with something positive. When you do this, you'll bring confidence and your peak performance to everything you do. You'll control your minds and create the feelings and experiences you want most in every area of your life.

*Action step:* **Listen to yourself.** We all know how important communication is. Employees who don't understand what you want can't enact your plan properly. Managers who misread your intention might act on what they think lies under your words. Even individuals who are close to us in other parts of our lives need clear information about what you mean or want.

You must apply that same clarity to yourself. Your internal communications must utilize the same approach as your external communications. To transmit messages clearly and effectively with your minds, you must first listen deeply to what your minds are telling you.

This doesn't mean listening to that chatter that crops up during the negative cascade. You have to push aside the "talking head," the commentator who sows panic and chaos in the cascade of your neural networks. Instead, track backward to the root cause. Listen deeply enough and you'll locate the story lodged in your database that is causing the mental chatter.

Sit somewhere quiet. Ask yourself, "When have I felt this way before?" Allow your mind to drift back to a situation that didn't go as planned. Work backward through individual events until you find the real point at which things went bad—the point where you recognize that a negative thought triggered a chaotic pattern: what thought did you have? Remember this point where your emotions were strongest: what emotions do you feel?

As you remember, you'll likely feel the same emotions that were present at that time. Good. Keep calm; take a few deep breaths and name the feelings as they occur. Become the acute observer. Then allow the subconscious mind to return to its work until you've pinpointed the initial cause.

This isn't difficult work. Observing the emotions feels difficult because your brain sends out those same neurochemicals when you remember an event. But since you're in a quiet place with complete control of your internal and external world, you'll be able to pause for however long you need to observe those emotions. Breathe into them. As you do, you'll find that each new emotion becomes easier to observe.

*Action step:* **You are not your emotions.** Once you've located the founding myth, recognize how that myth makes you feel. Since the emotions were created by erroneous information and neurochemicals, they are not set in stone. They are not like the heart, without which you cannot live. They are simply pathways that are supposed to ease your journey in life by providing you with ways to translate your current situation. You can choose to modify the pathway, upgrade to a different pathway or build an entirely new superhighway.

Emotions do serve a purpose. They act as signals for our fight-or-flight mechanism. They also allow you to feel joy, love, excitement and passion. Even the "negative" emotions like anger, grief, sadness and anxiety are simply signals that something needs your attention. Which is the whole point behind these chaotic patterns … something inside your database isn't working right. Be grateful you have these signals!

You'll continue to experience those same emotions until you fix whatever is wrong. Respect your feelings for what they are. Your subconscious mind has unique skills and special power; so do your emotions. But stop reliving your past. And that's exactly what happens whenever this chaotic pattern is triggered … you relive the same emotions, body responses and failure.

Study that past event. Note the emotions tied to the event without becoming attached to the feelings. All you're doing here is a systems analysis. When your distribution network fails, you don't become attached to the reason why it's failing. When your car breaks down, you don't panic while the mechanic diagnoses the problem. Your work here is no different. Emotions are not good or bad in and of themselves; they just are. Allow them to be, recognizing that you can harness them for peak performance.

*Action step:* **Fill the void.** To ensure that those chaotic patterns aren't replaced with similar stories, you must rewire your brain. Utilize the same visualization techniques discussed in the previous chapters. Bring your imagination into the mental game. See yourself living through that old story in a different way. Make your new choice. How do you act, think or feel differently? Create an outcome that generates confidence, joy and success.

Remember that once might not be enough. Those neural networks are physical; although you can immediately choose to change your mind, the neural pathways need time to rewire themselves. Repetition is the key. Imagine the same positive scenario over and over. Imagine new scenarios that generate the same emotions and the same level of results.

The neurons will fire in new patterns; each time they do, the new pathway is strengthened. Eventually the old neurons become weak, just like muscles you don't use. They will fade, and the strongest connections will become the new automatic pattern.

*Action step:* **Implement real-world change.** Back up this mental work with physical actions. The subconscious mind will recognize that you really mean what the conscious mind is telling it to do. It will be less likely to fall back on the old patterns and will make the transition more smoothly. Eventually your real-world actions will wipe out all trace of chaos, ensuring that no Trojans lurk in the network to pop up later.

Your physical actions don't have to be grandiose or complex to be effective. Psychologists have long assigned their patients a simple exercise: look in the mirror and smile. Even when you don't feel happy, the physical act of smiling tells your brain something different. Actually seeing yourself smile enhances the information. If you try this yourself, not only will you find that you're soon smiling for real, you might even end up laughing!

The body-brain feedback is that strong. Every action you perform with your body provides additional feedback to the subconscious mind. Even if you're worried about something, check your posture. Standing straight tells your brain something different: *I'm relaxed, I'm powerful, I am confident I will succeed.*

If you find that a particular business relationship isn't working out, do something about it. Have a conversation with that person or company. Be direct, honest and to the point. Communicate your goals for any change you're proposing, and see what happens. You might discover the other party felt the same unease and is happy to have the opportunity to change.

If the conversation doesn't generate the results you want, choose a different path. Change those things over which you have control. Assign that person a different task, one that best utilizes his or her unique skills. Switch the company to a different project, one on which it can do well, or change companies entirely. Any real-world action sends signals to your subconscious—now you're telling it to listen up!

Sometimes you can't take action on an overt level. So, change your perception. Choose to feel confident and assured when you deal directly with the poor situation. Be even-keeled. It won't serve you to become agitated or panicked over something you can't change. Accept the situation by bringing your best attitude to the table every time. You might never see any change in the external world, but that doesn't matter. What does matter is that you've made a change. It becomes easier for you to deal with poor situations, and it doesn't trigger a chaotic pattern.

## PAWS FOR REFLECTION

*Although some of your life events are quite serious,*
*they are all a process of evolution.*

*You evolve through your experiences,*
*whether you label them "good" or "bad."*

*Some of your greatest lessons come from what first*
*appears to be a negative experience.*

*Learn to grow with the ups and downs of life.*

*Knowledge + Experience + INsight = Wisdom* (to take action)

## CHEAT SHEET
# Choose Your Path

- A stream of automatic, unconscious, routine, familiar habits can cause confusion and errors in judgment.

- Automatic patterns are often considered negative because they generate chaos. You can choose to utilize the biology of your brain and rewire those neural networks. Your every thought and action will then be based on real connections and supportive emotions.

- The physical brain is adaptable. You can change the networks, clear out overgrowth or build entirely new networks to speed you on your way.

- Listen to yourself … deeply and with compassion. Allow yourself to release old feelings by sitting and fully experiencing them for however long is necessary. Then see the truth of the situation, and rewrite the outcome.

- Recognize that a chaotic pattern is telling you to pay attention. Something isn't right in your database. You need to go in and fix it.

- Create new automatic patterns by imagining a different outcome. Visualize a new story that brings you to a successful outcome or a peaceful place.

- Implement physical changes. No matter how large or small the action, the subconscious mind will register your commitment and seriousness, and it will accept the change more quickly.

- Recognize that sometimes you might not see a change in the external world. It doesn't matter. What does

## CHEAT SHEET

matter is that you have made a change and can deal with situations with a balanced internal strength that will only grow.

# Aim for the Peak

The air in the forest is crisp. Sambura, a majestic alpha wolf, runs circles inside a cage. Although his piercing blue eyes can see right into a man's soul, he now looks only for an opening, an escape. The fenced-in area has plenty of food and water, and his every medical need is tended. People arrive every day to care for him. Yet Sambura runs. He is here *for his own good*. Sambura runs.

The sound of his powerful paws against the earth is drowned out by the drumming in his chest. His heart cries for freedom. Sambura's mind races as fast as he runs. He never falters. He watches for any opening, any weakness in the fence. His tongue lolls from the effort. Sambura runs around and around and around.

Sometime over the next few weeks ... no one knows quite when ... Sambura loses his intensity. His head hangs, and he runs with his tail tucked between his legs. He is confused, agitated and highly stressed. He wants only one thing, to follow his heart. He wants to do what he is good at. Sambura wants to follow his passion, his natural instincts.

He adapts to the new environment but will never thrive in it. Each day the fire in his heart glows less and less. Soon it is just an ember. The fire is always there, though, haunting him. If he is ever set free, the fire will burn brightly. Until that day, Sambura runs.

## A Bigger Cage

You've achieved it all yet are unfulfilled. Vacations don't relieve the stress. A loving family doesn't eliminate the sorrow, grief or depression that gnaws at your mind like a wolf gnaws at the leg caught in a trap. Titles and money can't put a dent in that elusive feeling of dissatisfaction that circles you like a fence. You work harder, thinking the next achievement will wipe away all of those negative feelings. But nothing ever does.

Trust me. I've been there myself. Early in my career, I worked hard to learn all of the things I needed to improve my situation. I faced divorce, life as a single mother and the pitfalls of working in a male-dominated industry. It's easy to blame external sources for the sorrow: there's always something to point your finger at, something that becomes the scapegoat for your problems.

There are thrills, of course. You nail that million-dollar contract and the company flourishes. A hard-won promotion opens an entirely new career path. You give your family members everything they could possibly want or need, and your associates turn to you for help with their most important matters. Yet every time you reach a peak, you ask yourself why you aren't as happy as you think you should be.

External measures will never resolve internal issues. And until you address what's going on inside, your energy will always be scattered. You'll run circles, constantly hunting for a gap, a way to escape. You're in a cage, and you need to break free.

Life is like a roller coaster. Although some events and circumstances are serious, life itself is meant to be a fun ride. Every valley allows us to evolve and reach a new peak along the way. This diagram illustrates my philosophy for what happens between birth and physical death.

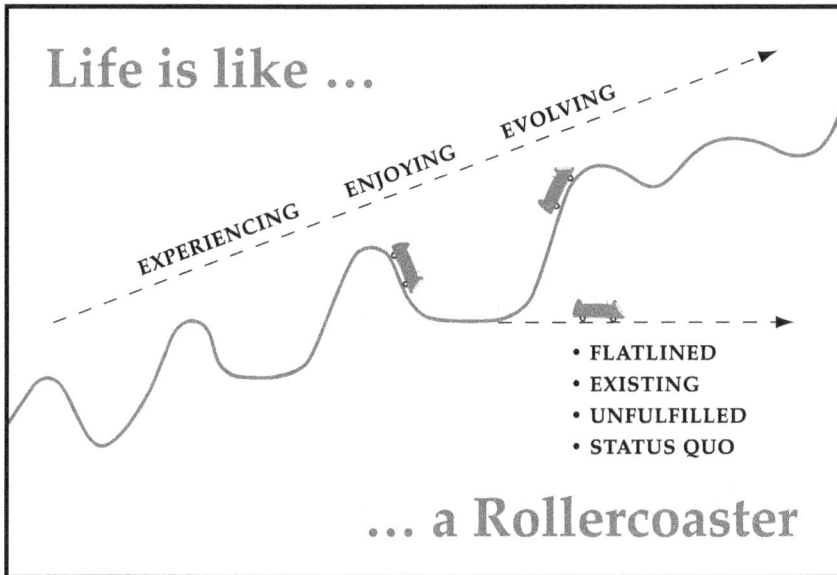

Life is like ...

EXPERIENCING — ENJOYING — EVOLVING

- FLATLINED
- EXISTING
- UNFULFILLED
- STATUS QUO

... a Rollercoaster

As the car goes up, up, up, you gaze at the blue sky, feel the sun on your face and the wind in your hair (if you have hair). You're gaining knowledge and experience. And the view is magnificent. The tracks run fast and easy as you laugh, learn, love and live. At the peak, you have a clear and unobstructed view of your life and what it means. Life is good!

Then the car begins to tip. You grab the bar and look for the brakes. But there's no steering wheel or stop button, no reverse gear to keep you from plunging off the peak. Screaming, arms flailing, you can only hope the car doesn't fly off the tracks. Even though your screaming and flailing add to the drama, they can't stop the plunge.

You finally reach the bottom. It's up to you to decide if the ride is over or if you want to continue with your evolution. This is where the best of your wisdom comes into play. You can choose to dwell in fear, grief, sadness, victimization, anger, shame, pain and all that negative stuff. Your mind, body and emotions will take the easy route and agree that it's too difficult to climb up again. Your literal subconscious mind, as always, will nod and say "OK!"

Your other choice is to acknowledge and accept what you're feeling and experiencing. I'm not saying you have to like it. I certainly didn't like it when my brother died. However, I did have to acknowledge and accept what I couldn't change. What had happened was over. The only thing I had control over was how I chose to feel about it. My thoughts were in my control … and feelings follow thoughts.

It took me twenty years to figure that out. When I finally got it, I changed the way I experienced every perceived downward slope after that. If it's already done and you can't change it, accept it. That's your first step back up the hill.

It's your first step toward freedom.

### Flatline

You might be thinking, "I don't want to feel, experience, or do (fill in the blank) again. It hurts too much. I don't know what to do to make it stop."

Guess what? Unless you face it (whatever "it" is), you'll continue to live it out in a stagnant way. I refer to this as flatlining. Because of this one decision, your life becomes a low-spirited existence with little excitement, meaning or passion. If you've flatlined, you're held captive by your subconscious thoughts and feelings. They crop up over and over again while you stay frozen under their power. You've fallen into a deep valley and have no desire to move upward.

Stay in this spot long enough and you'll begin to identify with your newly formed personality. You'll lose track of the real you; and the part you're currently playing—that "dude playing a dude disguised as another dude"—will take over. You're like the wolf that is captured by a fence he neither understands nor can fight. No matter how many times you run that circle, a gap will never appear. You'll never break free. Your world has become about existing, not about living.

One day I left a movie theater and sat in my car. I don't remember what movie I'd seen, but I can still feel the panic and intensity of that moment. My eyes welled up with tears. My twenty-two-year relationship with my husband had just ended.

I let out a primal scream. Then the accusations began: "It's all his fault! No, it's all my fault!" The tears fell faster, and my emotions swirled like a summer thunderstorm. I could hardly catch my breath. My heart was punching through my ribs, and my stomach hurt.

*What am I supposed to do now?* I wondered. *What should I have done differently? How am I ever going to hold it all together?* And on … and on … and on.

I finally pulled down the visor to clean my face. I didn't want my two kids to see me this way. As I looked in the mirror, my eyes came to a pinpoint focus. I immediately stopped crying. After a few moments, I closed my eyes. I'm so tired of crying, I thought. This isn't getting me anywhere.

Thus began my journey from fear into freedom.

It wasn't his fault or my fault. Our feelings simply changed. Though we loved each other, we were no longer in love with each other. The decision was mutual. That left me on my own with two children to raise. Fear had sent me spiraling around in a useless circle of grief and despair.

You might be experiencing fear right now. You might want to leave your job or a relationship—but fear is holding you back. Maybe you're afraid to tackle a new goal or create a vision of your lifelong ambition. Maybe you can't bring yourself to ride that monster roller coaster again. Maybe you're afraid of becoming too powerful, too successful or too happy because then you'll have a lot to lose.

Fear affects us all. Our bodies shiver or we perspire. Tension fills our limbs and our minds. Sleep won't come even though we're exhausted. And our thoughts are overpowered with "talking heads," the internal voices that are so good at holding us back and pinning us down. Our theoretical stories grow out of proportion as we second-guess our every thought, desire and need.

The distance between a stagnant existence and success is the length of a single step. You can choose to live in the world of "I can't" or you can choose to step into the fear and move through it.

I drove home that day, grabbed a pencil and drew up a detailed plan for how to get what I wanted out of life. My list included providing a good life and education for my children; selling my house; trading my IROC for a more practical and less expensive Honda; rebuilding myself financially; and taking my career to the next level.

That was twenty years ago. Today my daughter and son are happy, healthy and doing great things. My life is filled with adventure. Fear still creeps in at times … and I always meet it head-on. My experience gave me the wisdom to help myself whenever new situations threatened to cage me with sorrow or fear. I've also been able to help others break free of their own emotional cages.

I once worked with an internationally known speaker, writer and coach. Somewhere along the way, he'd lost confidence in his ability to connect with his audience. Fear was building up inside him, and he was being very hard on himself. Because he'd been enormously successful, he held high expectations for his own ability to get things done.

With my help, he found the truth … his truth. He reconnected to the truth of who he was and the place from which his strength came. He found that his courage had never really disappeared; it had died down to an ember but had always glowed, waiting for the Alpha Leader of his mind to fan it back into life.

He quickly regained his confidence and his ability to connect with people. Instead of chastising himself, he became aware of his thoughts. He learned how to shift them away from negative, self-criticizing chatter to positive support. Fear gave way to courage and trust. Today he continues to wow people around the world.

It's easy to get caught up inside the self-made fences of daily life. Dates, commitments and promises each add another section to the fence. If you're running on autopilot in repetitive patterns, you might feel that colleagues, clients, friends and family, even society, have more control over your life than you. Your spark has smoldered. You feel confused, stressed and agitated, wanting to escape, hungry to ignite that ember into a full-blown fire.

There is another choice. Acknowledge and accept the experience and your feelings. Welcome it all. You don't have to like it; you do have to accept it. The only thing you can control is how you choose to feel about it. Your thoughts are in your control. You are the Alpha Leader of your minds, remember?

### Flatlining on the Job

You're strategically planning your department's annual budget, cash projections and performance goals. Normally you start by laying out the goals. Your linear mind tallies up the people, equipment and percentages required to incrementally grow your department. Finally, after much deliberation, you put the plan together.

It's certainly important to think things through. What you end up with is nice, analytical … and boring. The answers were based on your past experience and your personal database. You pegged certain individuals with certain tasks, assigned duties based on past departmental performance and maximized the use of every resource at your disposal. The plan is efficient and effective … to a point.

Here's what it won't do: It won't generate new ideas. It won't find new ways to supercharge your available resources for even better results. It won't find the hidden talents in your team members and boost their productivity beyond previous abilities. You might end up making the fence a little bigger, but the company still will be in a cage.

That's because you relied only on one mind. You used only your logical thoughts. You applied a calculator that assessed, measured, delineated and limited your options. You left no room for imagining beyond what, in the past, had been reasonable and possible. So how's that working for you? You've flatlined the task, your company and yourself.

You can change the scenario. Add your imagination.

Help your subconscious mind join the meeting by setting up an image: It's December 31, and your department has experienced an amazingly creative, productive and prosperous year. What happened? What did your team do differently this year? How did you communicate and cooperate with each other? What benchmarks did you reach? What new processes did you implement? What new inventions or products did you create?

As answers appear, bring in your emotions. What are your peers saying about you and your department? Hear their exact words. What are your staff members saying? What specifically are they thanking you for? Listen well, and take in their words. What do you say in return? Express your gratitude with deep feelings and words from your heart.

Now ask, "What's the easiest way to accomplish this?" "What steps need to be taken?" Before long, answers will pour in. Write them down or record them to capture everything as quickly as possible. Once you're done, reengage your analytical mind. As you create the rest of the plan, it will naturally support your imagined outcome.

Now you're no longer flatlining. Now you're climbing higher still. You're enjoying the ever-changing view, anticipating the new peak that will itself lead to another prosperous climb. And everyone else in the other cars—your staff and the company, your coworkers and family—are also enjoying the ride. With your imagination, there are no more fences. You've broken free and the internal flame is burning bright.

## Change the Scenario

Imaginative leaders create the roadmap for others to follow. By using your imagination, you generate a clear edge that can set you and your company apart from your competition.

Conceive it, believe it, achieve it—it's up to you to figure out what your "it" is. Fortunately, it can be discovered through your imagination.

Albert Einstein once said imagination is more important than knowledge. Imagination breaks through barriers and moves leadership strategies to the next level. All great leaders, inventors, scientists, architects, engineers and athletes use imagination to their best advantage.

Everything humans have come to depend on sprang from someone's imagination, such as the chair you sit on, the house where you live, and the clothes you wear. And even the uses of invisible energy waves such as we find in microwaves, cell phones, the Internet, and your iPod, sprang from somebody's imagination.

Somehow, the class called "How to Use Your Imagination" got left off the typical school curriculum. Children are naturally curious; they're meant to be. They constantly ask, "Why?" At some point, their parents or teachers hit the tipping point of their patience. The children are hushed. The imagination is stifled early on. When you reconnect with this tool, your world can change.

For athletes, plugging into their imaginations can make the difference between second place and first. Michael Phelps, winner of an unprecedented eight gold medals at the 2008 Olympic Games, said, "Nothing is impossible. With so many people saying it couldn't be done, all it takes is an imagination."

Using your imagination works even better when you add emotions to your visual images. The idea is to get your linear mind out of the way and to fully power up your creative frontal lobe. Then you hold onto the new image by charging it with intense emotional energy.

In the fall of 2007, I had an opportunity to put my own visualizations to the test. When my friends heard I was planning a great-white-shark dive, they thought I was crazy. "Why would any sane person get in a cage surrounded by great whites?" they asked. "Are you nuts? Didn't you see *Jaws?*"

For me it was an opportunity to experience something new. The Isle de Guadalupe is surrounded by cold water and visited by sea lions. Every fall, the great whites congregate there to feed. I was practically guaranteed to see these powerful creatures up close and personal, and in a feeding frenzy. I was excited … right up until fear charged in.

It was time to evoke my imagination. For several weeks beforehand, I imagined the perfect trip: lots of large sharks, a safe and professional crew, amazing opportunities for pictures and my safe return. I even talked to the sharks, thanking them for allowing me to come safely into their waters to experience their beauty and power. I also imagined my son-in-law, Martin, and me on a plane heading home to Phoenix. I felt our excitement and heard our conversations as we retold our stories.

It worked. When my turn came up to be in the cage for an hour, I was excited. My first sighting caused me to scream into my regulator with the ultimate thrill of being eye to eye with a Great White. I was within arm's length of these magnificent predators. Twelve feet, fourteen feet … they were huge!

Had I listened to the voices or bought into my fear, I might have cancelled. Instead, my imagination replaced my fear with courage and trust. Because of that, my experience was amazing.

The key to receiving answers is to get out of your head and

into your imagination. If your thinking mind could solve the problem, it would have figured it out by now. You can't keep doing what you've been doing and expect new and different results. That's Einstein's definition of insanity.

Knowing how imperative action is to achieving ever-greater success, I gently (and sometimes not so gently) nudge my clients to take action beyond what they consider reasonable and possible. I love to encourage them to use their imaginations to expand their databases and explore new possibilities. Based on my experience, knowledge and insight with others, I know they'll be rewarded—and so will you.

Once you take action, you're back on the roller coaster, climbing up again. Your spirit soars as you evolve, experience and enjoy. No flatlining. No smoldering embers. As you reach the top, you have yet another unique opportunity to view life with insight and to determine what's true for you. Great wisdom is yours and will continue to serve you day after day. You won't have to break through the fence. When you use your imagination, the cage won't even exist.

### The Power of Being Fully Present

Everybody knows different things. We can sit around and impress each other with facts and statistics. We enthusiastically share our knowledge and receive new knowledge in return. This is a form of evolution. It increases your cache of information and expands your database. It can also change your perceptions. Knowledge is the first part of the equation:

**Knowledge + Experience + INsight = Wisdom** (to take action).

Experience creates a memory in your body's cellular makeup. When we learn through experience, the impression is branded deeper in our memory banks because greater levels of emotions are tied to the thoughts. These memories live forever. You can recall them any time you choose and relive the thrills and triumphs.

When you add insight, you can examine your knowledge and experiences to discover what they mean to you. You can then choose to continue certain experiences. You can also choose to never again experience others. You are the boss of you. Using insight, the Alpha Leader determines what the mind holds onto and what it releases.

Together, the three create wisdom.

Your past holds great memories and lessons. This database is incredibly useful. It can be a great place to visit, but you don't want to live there. The specific events stored there can also generate self-sabotaging automatic patterns. Although the choice to take on the thoughts and emotions associated with being trapped has always been yours, you might never have been taught how to use your mind to generate a different outcome.

Today, you've reached another juncture of choice. You can keep doing what you've been doing, thinking how you've been thinking, and experiencing the same emotional upheaval. Or you can take control of your thoughts and emotions by staying awake, aware and alert. Recognize when sabotaging thoughts creep in. Know that the thoughts are based on prior experiences, the emotions connected to those experiences and fears about the future.

The present is the only place you have power. When you remember the past or imagine the future, you do so in your present state of awareness. When you develop a heightened sense of awareness, you catch all the sabotaging thoughts, emotions and actions before they catch you. Determine which thoughts, emotions and actions serve you, and focus on them. Identify what's moving you forward and what's holding you back.

Take your power back right here and now. It's a clear choice. Allow your base of wisdom to expand into action. Action is a powerful and essential part of being a strong leader. As the leader of yourself, your edge comes from living in the now. By experiencing the now, you can dictate exactly what that experience will be.

Your future can be something that causes you to worry. Remember that you create exactly what you focus on. Why focus on what you *don't* want? A low level of anxiety has a purpose, of course. It tells you something needs your attention. So figure out what the problem is, and correct it. Action is the only way to ensure the dreaded event doesn't occur. Action propels you into increasingly better circumstances where you can perform at your peak and generate optimal success.

Imagine your future strategically, professionally and joyfully, and you'll naturally create your future strategically, professionally and joyfully. Imagination is the beginning of all great things. By using it as a tool, you can create your new vision and focus on the result you want. You have the power to go beyond what you currently believe is reasonable and possible. When you do, you'll enjoy the exciting roller-coaster ride that comes with being the leader of the pack.

### WOLF WAY #4: Continue to Climb

Acceptance of your situation, no matter how bad, will stop the downward spiral and keep you from flatlining. Once you accept what's true, become the inquisitive observer. Remove the emotional charge attached to the event, and engage your subconscious mind. You'll generate creative solutions your conscious, linear mind could never imagine.

As answers emerge, take action. Answers without action only provide you with information. All the information in the world is useless without action.

*Action step:* **Muscle testing.** You're going to prove the power of being fully present. You can do this with someone's help or on your own. Once you believe that your power is in the present time, you'll spark that ember into a fire that will propel you through the rest of these action steps.

Stand up. Center yourself with your feet shoulder-width apart. Close your eyes and relax. When you feel balanced and calm, think about some past event where you were happy. Imagine yourself on vacation or at a party.

Holding that memory clearly in your mind, extend your arm out to one side. Ask your assistant to press down on your arm using two fingers. Resist the pressure as much as you can without letting go of the memory. If you prefer to do this alone, you can try to lift a phone book off your desk with one hand.

If you're resisting your assistant, note how far down he or she is able to press your arm. If you're picking up the phone book, notice how difficult or easy it is to lift. Now center yourself again, and think of something you have planned for the future. Again, be sure to choose a pleasant experience, something you anticipate with joy. Repeat the same action, noting how far your arm goes down or how heavy the phone book feels.

Center yourself a final time. For this step, open your eyes. Take a moment to look around. Notice the color of the light in the room and the placement of the furniture. Smell the trace of shampoo in your hair, and feel the temperature of the air on your skin. Maintaining that awareness of your surroundings, repeat the exercise.

You'll be shocked. Your arm won't go down nearly as much or nearly as easily. The phone book will feel half its actual weight. Because you are awake, alive and aware of the present moment, you have increased your physical power. And since that level of power is generated by your mental state, your thoughts will be charged with the same increased power.

*Action step:* **Ask the right questions.** Learn to ask questions that support the outcome you're looking to achieve. Sitting alone, first use your conscious mind to name what you're thinking and the emotions you're experiencing. If your current thoughts and feelings are not serving your needs, what would? Your goals may be clarity, happiness, prosperity, courage, creativity or a better job. Write down your goals.

*Action step:* **Access your imagination.** Now bring your imagination into play. The key to engaging your subconscious mind is to get out of your head and into your heart. First, stop the static. Close your eyes to block out external stimuli. Close the door to your office to cut off the sounds of people chatting in the halls. Shut off your phone, and cut the email alert on your computer.

Now calm the waters. Take five slow, deep breaths. Be sure to breathe in from your belly using the diaphragm muscle. Hold it for a comfortable few seconds. Then release it slowly and evenly. Image a gentle ocean wave that is washing over your mind and body, pulling all the tension out to sea.

Now take an emotional time-out. Imagine yourself looking down from that thirty-thousand-foot level. Simply observe. Do not participate emotionally; suspend all judgment.

Create two lists: For the first list, ask yourself what you will gain if you step into your fear. Will you feel some type of pleasure? Will you feel pride, joy, triumph? Will you have these feelings even if you eventually fail, knowing that you tried? Write it down. Then, for the second list, ask what you'll lose if you stagnate. How might it hurt you? How will you feel … sad, depressed, frustrated, angry? Will you feel defeated because you never tried? Write that down.

You are engaging both your minds. As your thoughts clarify, the process takes you out of the emotional framework and places you squarely in an intellectual frame of mind. Your conscious mind asks questions, and your subconscious mind produces answers. One guides; the other follows. One analyzes; the other emotes. Take as long as you need to fully delve into every aspect of your subconscious. Allow the conscious mind all of the time it needs to pinpoint the meaning of each answer.

*Action step:* **Generate a plan.** Examine your lists. Create a plan. Now make a choice. Are you going to stagnate, or are you going to take action? Choose which action to take. Remember, you have the power. If you've decided to take action, keep moving through any negative emotions that may arise. Every action step you take will move you further away from your past entrapments and closer to your intended goal. Set benchmarks and timelines for each of the steps necessary to accomplish your new goal.

Use your imagination here, as well. Remember that you can't keep doing things the old way if you want to generate different results. Connect your resources in new ways to achieve new results. Be specific. Determine exactly who will help you and what they'll do. Picture the machines, money and tools you'll need along the way.

Be just as specific with your emotions. Feel every new thrill as things come together, and celebrate the joy of having accomplished each milestone. Visualize your successes and your triumphs. Push past what you thought possible before, to create an astonishing, prosperous future. Then implement your plan in the now … your moment of power.

As you implement this plan, stay flexible. Allow the new experiences to generate new opportunities. Just because you didn't plan them doesn't mean they aren't valid, viable options!

## PAWS FOR REFLECTION

*Repeat it, believe it, then live it.*

## CHEAT SHEET

# Aim for the Peak

- Life is like a roller coaster. Every time you hit a valley, you choose whether to get off or keep going. If you refuse to continue, you'll flatline.

- The distance between stagnation and success is the length of a single step.

- Everyone faces fear. Everyone gets caught up in their emotional traps. The only thing you control is how you choose to think and thus how you feel.

- Using only your conscious, linear mind at work (or in any other area of life) means you'll flatline.

- Use your imagination to expand your database, explore new possibilities and climb to the next peak.

- You can't keep doing things the same way and expect change. Use your imagination to find new paths and generate fresh opportunities. Go beyond what you thought possible before!

- Knowledge + Experience + INsight = Wisdom (to take action).

- Your past is gone and the future is always at least a day away. Remaining in the past or future weakens your body and mind. Your place and time of power is now.

- Benchmarks and timelines still apply. Your conscious mind charts the new path generated by your imagination.

**Free tools at www.HowlLeadership.com**
*(Use VIP Code: ALPHA)*

# Remember Your Instincts

Wolves often use body language to communicate. To us, the spectacular display of fangs and trembling lips conveys deadly anger. We'd sure as heck get out of that alpha's way! But wolf communication is far more complex than we might first assume. A host of messages are conveyed through subtle adjustments only the keen human observer might catch.

Tail position is a perfect example. Within the pack, a wolf that holds its tail high is presenting as dominant. Lower-ranking wolves hold their tails down. Stiff tails are a sign of anxiety; danger is present inside or outside of the pack, so the wolves are gearing up for action. Tails that wag are clearly a sign of welcome and joy.

The wolf is very expressive, and ear positioning is important. A high tail is usually accompanied by upright ears to capture every sound. Lower-ranking wolves keep their heads down and their ears back. When danger threatens, the ears swivel forward to pinpoint the threat. And when fear takes over, the tail is tucked between the legs and the ears lie flat.

This kind of communication goes on all the time. Even when wolves are at rest, you can easily tell who's who in the "Wolf Pack Hall of Fame." The alpha might not stand at the physical center of the pack every moment, but it really is the center of its society. Every other wolf constantly looks over to check in with the leader. Any movement by the alpha is a call to action—to remain relaxed, to confront danger, to begin the hunt or even to play.

Everything wolves do is energetic. Every movement of tails and ears signals an individual's state of mind and triggers responses in the rest of the pack. By remaining aware of their surroundings, any change in the environment or the pack is immediately transmitted by body language. Through this ingrained communication, the individuals work together for the good of all.

### Energy at Work

Remember that your brain is an electrical thunderstorm. Neurons are firing every second to help you find solutions at work and enjoy that TV program at home. Every thought is a form of energy. We are energy, and everything around us is energy.

Dr. Bruce H. Lipton, a cellular biologist, says in his website article based on the wisdom of the cells, "*Everything* is giving off energy. As we are doing neurological processing of the world that we live in, including our thoughts and beliefs, we are actually creating a magnetic vibration, like a tuning fork that emanates from our head out into the field."

What you think matters. It impacts your energy—the magnetic vibration you give off that others pick up on. It's not something you can see, touch or hear, but it's as effective and efficient as a wolf's tail position. However, wolves don't consciously decide to lift their tails or swivel their ears;

they automatically do these things because they are living a particular role: an alpha or a beta, a leader or a follower. Their body language conveys their position because it's who they are; it's their energy.

Yes, that all sounds very Zen. Yet this is straight-up science, the cutting edge of physics that has opened windows into quarks and superpositioning and string theory. Don't worry: I'm not going to babble about chanting *or* cosmology! I am, however, going to talk about the very real way our world works. Since you exist in that world and are made of the same material and energetic forms, the lessons apply equally to you.

Consider light. Waves moving at different frequencies are picked up by our eyes as different colors. Those moving at lower frequencies create red, orange and yellow, while higher frequencies register as blue and violet. Frequencies are vibrational patterns. Vibrations are pure energy that happens to show up in different forms by moving in different ways.

You learned that back in grade school. You also learned about the molecule, the basic building block of all material things. Each molecule contains a nucleus, and a certain number of protons and/or electrons circle the core. Putting hydrogen and oxygen together in one way yields a water molecule; add just one more oxygen molecule, and you have hydrogen peroxide.

Yet it's not enough to simply know the formula for a particular compound. C2H6O, for example, is a single formula that identifies two very different substances. One is the ethyl alcohol found in beer or wine, which can be quite pleasant to consume. The other is methyl ether, a toxic substance commonly used as a refrigerant. You wouldn't want to serve that to your dinner guests!

Since the compounds are the same and are present in the same quantity, something outside of their physical properties makes the formulation different. That something is energy. The electromagnetic field, the interaction between individual particles, is what creates the particular molecule. The bond between the different components determines whether the molecule is flammable or inert, whether it's malleable or solid, and even how readily it can link with other molecules to create entirely new materials.

Since your body is made up of molecules, all the same rules apply to you. The receptors in your nose are made of molecules shaped to fit with odor molecules emitted by chocolate and coffee and flowers and car exhaust. The molecules in your red blood cells are shaped to fit with oxygen so it can be carried to every part of your body. And since the particles in each molecule are constantly spinning around the nucleus, you are made almost entirely of energy in motion.

**Start with Energy**

Have you ever thought, *This doesn't feel right* … and it wasn't? As a leader, it's important to listen to those inner whispers. Often we call this a gut reaction or a hunch. Just as your five senses are meant to process information so you can evolve, your intuition serves much the same purpose. Call it what you like, but know that your gut reaction, hunch or intuition can save your business. It might even save your life.

When I owned my construction company, I taught a course I created called "The Spirit of Entrepreneurial Leadership™" to my upper- and middle-management teams. In one of our weekly meetings, I spoke about the intuitive inner voices that provide guidance. During the following week, my managers were supposed to listen to their intuition and take action on it.

At our next meeting, one vice president shared his story. While driving on the freeway, he'd heard an inner voice telling him to move over. It took him a minute to realize what he'd heard and to change lanes. Seconds later, a mattress flew off the back of the pickup truck he'd been behind. If he hadn't listened and taken action, that mattress would have hit his car. The consequences could have been devastating.

Trust your intuition. Don't dismiss it. Your gut reaction is just that … your body responding to what it intuitively knows to be true or false. If your gut is queasy, tight or just not right, the thought you're having or decision you're about to make probably isn't right, either.

Your body provides you with a wealth of information. When you're enthusiastic about something, you feel energized. Your stride is confident and self-assured; your head is up, and you're tuned in to your surroundings. When something's off, your body knows. You feel weighed down with the flaw. You'll walk differently, and your voice won't be as strong. That energy will prevent you from focusing on the tasks at hand. Until you pinpoint the problem, the flaw will keep nagging at your body. Your mind won't function at its full capacity.

My personal practice is to gather all of the information I possibly can, come up with my best plan of action and then sit for a moment to see how I feel. I've walked away from million-dollar contracts because my intuition told me it wasn't a good deal for my company. It might have been a good deal for someone else, just not for my company.

Your team will pick up on that energy. They'll feel a change; they'll know you're not as confident about this deal or this program. They'll lose their own ability to function at peak performance, because your anxiety will become theirs. They'll also wonder why you're going down this road if you're unsure of the outcome. That shakes their confidence in your leadership, your ability to create what's in the best interest of the entire pack.

So listen to that internal voice. Check in with your body, and see what your physical energy is telling you. Remember other times when you didn't listen to your subconscious, when you allowed the logical mind to overwhelm the gut with reams of facts in support of your path. Hindsight allows you to locate the flaw you couldn't see back then; it also proves that you should be listening to those hunches.

### Energy in Action

Awareness of your energy is a great foundation, but it's only the start. Remember that action is as important a part of the wisdom formula as any other part. Without action, you've only got a bunch of data sitting in your brain. A wolf who knows all the best hunting techniques is useless if she never actually goes hunting. The pack won't follow her because even though the beta wolf is less capable overall, at least he brings down game.

Take action. Utilize everything stored in your leadership toolbox. Direct your energy, and influence that of others, for the greatest gain. This can be done internally or externally, by changing your attitude or by energizing your team with your own passion and enthusiasm. There are also steps you can take to change the energy patterns, the frequencies, of your pack. It's as simple as how you walk into a room.

Before a weekly management meeting, I paused to whisper to the receptionist. "I'm going to yell at you in a minute,"

I said, "and then slam the door to the conference room. It's just a game, I don't really mean it. Just play along."

She knew my quirks well enough to go with the flow. I waited another few minutes until the start time for the meeting had passed. I wanted everyone to have time to engage in a little social activity while they waited. When I finally approached the conference room, I could hear my managers exchanging stories and laughing. They were all kicked back in their chairs looking very relaxed.

Stopping dead in front of the receptionist, I took a deep breath. "I told you I needed that call!" I yelled. "I don't know what you were thinking. I can't depend on you for anything!"

I briskly walked into the conference room, slammed the door, and plopped into my chair. After a pause, I calmly said, "So, what's up guys? Who wants to start?"

"What's wrong?" one asked.

"Nothing. Come on, let's go. Who wants to start?"

Every one of them sat ramrod straight. Their eyes were down, and their shoulders were tight. Complete silence filled the room. Their enthusiasm and easy interaction had been destroyed with the slam of the door.

I finally whispered, "How do you feel right now?"

"What do you mean?" they asked. "What's wrong with you?"

A hint of a grin touched my lips. Suddenly they realized they'd been sucked into my game.

"Who felt what?" I asked. "What changed in the energy of the room? How did your bodies react differently? What was going through your heads? Could you even think straight?"

That's all it took. They'd had a live experience of being caught in a wave of negative energy. We had a great discussion. Everyone noted how heavy the atmosphere in the room had become. They had barely been able to look at me for fear of what might have happened because of the missed phone call. Their fear was not of me but of the thoughts running through their head. Their bodies had immediately become tense. They lost their ability to think straight. They unconsciously had gone into fight-or-flight mode.

That's exactly how our minds and bodies are designed to work. It's primal and immediate. Had it been a real event, my teams would have been out of commission for some time. A few individuals might have carried that energy for days. For others, the experience might have triggered memories of similar past events. The results would have been lost productivity, poor quality and decreased creativity.

Do your actions, commands, or energy levels ever shut down your peers or pack? Have you ever been on the receiving end and experienced that automatic shutdown yourself? It's not fun. It's certainly not effective.

When you walk through the door of your building or office, check your attitude at the door. If someone cut you off during your commute or a disturbing phone call put you in a foul mood, shift your energy before you affect the rest of the office. Remain aware of your thoughts, emotions and actions. As a leader, *you* set the tone. Pick your energy wisely for the benefit of yourself and your pack.

After my little game, my managers made a group decision. The minute we put our hand on the front door, we would check our attitude. The front door became our trigger to remember. Every day, we would bring our best to the office and set the example for everyone else.

Within a week, one VP slipped up. Andy was within earshot of my office. He was chastising one of his project coordinators in a public space. When I silently waved him into my office, he knew he'd forgotten the lesson.

"So, Andy," I asked, "how do you think Kathy feels right now? Did you notice that accounting got up and shut their office door? And look—the other project coordinator is now consoling Kathy. What's wrong with this picture?"

Andy had tried to address a problem. Instead, he'd quite effectively shut down productivity in his department and others. Because he'd distracted so many people, his actions possibly caused quality control to diminish. He also lost the respect of many people in the company. It took time to gain all of it back. The words lasted seconds; the energy rippled for hours and beyond.

He and I remembered how important it is to stay awake, aware and alert. His actions were an example of how internal energy can affect others. The meeting game shows how external energy can impact everyone in a room, everyone within earshot. Since leaders are always at the center of their pack, every nuance of their stance is the focus of all others. Energy oscillates in different patterns; be sure your energy is tuned to the exact frequency you need to generate maximum results.

If we become unaware of our thoughts, emotions and actions, it can affect many people. It takes only seconds to have that impact and much longer to undo its effects. Always be aware of your own frequency, the energy you're sending out into the world. Check in regularly with your body, your actions and your words. Know what you're about to do, and adjust the flow to create peak performance in your pack.

## Your Body Says It All

Your body talks to others as much as it talks to you. Wolves communicate nonverbally all the time. After a fight, the loser demonstrates submission by lying on its back and showing its belly and throat. The winner bares its fangs. Wolves also play in silence. This is their way of practicing for the hunt when silence is imperative. Raised hackles, a loose tail, body bumps to greet returning members and nips all communicate different messages.

As a leader, you give off physical signals all the time. You stride into a conference room and sit at the head of the table to assert your dominance. You meet a person's gaze when he or she asks a tough question. Your handshake is firm, and your gestures propel your team into action. You are teaching new things and reaffirming old knowledge through nonverbal behaviors.

Your pack will always believe your behaviors, even when your words don't match. You can talk up your excitement about the new contract you've just signed, blathering on about profit margins and resource integration. Yet, the whole time, your leg is bouncing and you're wringing your hands. Your staff isn't listening to your words; they're listening to your body. Their minds are registering all the subconscious signals of panic, lack of confidence and anxiety. Your concerns become theirs, even if no one knows what the concerns are.

You listen to other people's bodies, as well. When a member of your staff arrives late and says a traffic accident delayed him, your mind notices how wrinkled his forehead is as he tries to convince you. When a colleague adamantly claims she's open to new ideas, you see how her arms wrap defensively across her chest. You ask a question, and the answer is yes while the head shakes no. You don't know what's wrong, but clearly something is.

I believe the body before I believe the words. I've rejected job candidates based on their handshake. One woman almost took me to my knees with her grip. Though her way of addressing me was congenial and she had plenty of talent, I knew she wouldn't fit our culture. Her body was telling me something that was truer than anything she could say. In time, I knew her domineering qualities would show up.

Alternately, I've interviewed project managers who talked a good story yet their handshake was weak. When I pushed just a bit, they crumbled. I look for people whose knowledge connects with their follow-through. Someone making decisions that affect my bottom line must have inner confidence, strength and conviction . . . not simply an outward show. The subconscious mind might be the only part to register these patterns, but they're as real as the molecules in our bodies.

The impact of body language might not be news to you. When you extend the same lesson to all your actions, though, you will reap even greater rewards. While I was still in construction, I threw an annual banquet to show my employees how much I appreciated their hard work throughout the year. Since I wanted to really get the message across, I chose the best place in town.

Sounds wonderful, doesn't it? Well, it was a mistake. Although the managers were happy with the fine dining experience, many of the employees were less than comfortable. They felt constrained by the setting and didn't bond as well as they might have if the dinner had been held somewhere else. The lesson hit home when one gentleman had to borrow a suit jacket just to get in the door.

I didn't want anyone to be turned away. This wasn't about dressing up and feeling posh; it was about celebrating as a team. How much can anyone celebrate if they're wondering which fork to use or whether their clothes are good enough? That kind of situation generates heavy, negative energy. That's the exact opposite of what I'd intended. We changed the venue the following year and had roaring good fun … as intended.

Everything you do generates a particular energy. Bring your knowledge of your pack's needs into the decision process. When faced with an issue, be creative about finding solutions that will benefit everyone. Sure, filet mignon might impress more people than barbeque in the park. However, the impression can backfire, generating negative energy rather than the positive vibrations you need to carry you forward.

**Yip, Howl and Growl**

Wolves have a language all their own. They whine, howl, growl and yip at different levels of intensity depending on what they are communicating. When two wolves meet, the higher-ranking one snarls to force the other wolf to accept its place. Puppies cry when approached by the female to convey their hunger. And a pack at a carcass is a cacophony of growls that warn low-ranking wolves to wait their turn.

How wonderfully we'd all communicate if we were more like wolves. Yet, so often, humans talk about what they don't want. Recently I overheard one person ask another where he would like to go for dinner. The response was, "Well, I don't want fast food. And I really don't like Italian. I don't want to get dressed up or go out too late."

What part of that response really answered the question? This type of communication creates a lack of clarity.

Questions and answers must be bantered back and forth before the issue can be resolved. Let's say you ask your home sales team what might attract more customers and what you hear is this:

> "They don't like long lead times."

> "They get angry if their home isn't on schedule."

> "One customer balked at not being able to see some of the options before signing the contract."

Now, you can extrapolate a more direct answer from these statements, but you'll still be in almost-maybe territory. Are you close to what clients really want or still far off base? Look at the second statement as an example. Does this mean that a large percent of homes your company delivers are not on schedule, or is this person smarting from having delivered his last home late?

Who knows? *Who cares?* You're not getting answers; you're getting opposite answers, the reverse of what you asked for. Opposite answers are a waste of time. Teach your pack and yourself to be direct. State what *is*, instead of what's *not*.

Remember, too, that words are energy. Just like light waves, sound waves vibrate at certain frequencies. Our voices can become heavy with emotion, slow when we're thoughtful and fast when we're excited. Every word carries some of that energy out into the world: when you talk about what you don't want, your focus attracts what you don't want!

We're back to how the subconscious impacts our conscious thoughts. Every time the first sales person sees a potential customer who isn't well dressed, he thinks, *This one's going to be a waste of time. She isn't going to buy a house from us. She can't afford this area.* During the pitch, he might say all of the right things, follow protocol to the letter and then prove his theory right when the potential home buyer looks somewhere else.

When the second sales person sees the same potential home buyer, she gets excited. Her inner and outer communication resonates with positive energy. *Alright, here we go—another happy home buyer. She's dressed comfortably so she can spend time looking for the perfect home. I can provide it.* During the pitch she is sincere and caring, and she helps the potential customer imagine herself in the home. She closes the deal.

Both sales people took the same amount of time, presented the exact same homes and followed the same protocol. Yet the second person repeatedly ranks top in sales. She creates an energy, an expectation, an intention of making a sale. She knows it's a game of percentages, and her numbers go up because she sees and experiences every customer as a buyer. Customers pick up on it. They buy into it without even realizing what is happening.

Energy attracts like energy. The man who sets his intent on what he doesn't want—that is, to waste time—creates exactly that … buyers who fiddle around. The sales person has limited the negotiation from the start: *Buy quickly or don't work with me.* By focusing on time, he has distracted himself from the goal of selling. He has limited his client pool to only those individuals who are in a hurry to buy. Of course his numbers are low!

As a leader, stay alert to the conversation that's going on in your head. Listen to what your pack members are saying. Set your intention toward a positive goal. Generate possibilities without limits, without the subconscious thoughts created by past failures. It affects your mind, your results and your bottom line.

## WOLF WAY #5: Generates Real Results through Real Action

Information without action is as useful as an alpha that won't hunt. You can generate brilliant ideas, but if you never implement the plan, you'll never succeed. You must constantly move forward and continue to climb that hill to achieve your next peak. The energy of both your actions and your intentions will propel you and your company toward your present goals and future success.

*Action step:* **Integrate your intuition.** Pick some decision you need to make soon. Pull out all the files related to this decision, and scan them quickly. Take special note of the benefits that will accrue if you choose to proceed down this path. Then think of another potential path and its specific benefits. Note the pitfalls involved in each—additional costs, the strain on resources, the pressures each timeline will create for your staff.

Now close the files. Sit quietly and stare at a blank space on the wall or out your window. Notice anything different in your body as you think separately about each possible choice. Are you leaning forward, anticipating the benefits one path can offer? Does your hand clench whenever you think about the potential for cost overruns that might ensue after a different decision?

Maybe it's something as simple as a slightly increased heartbeat or a gentle flush of pleasure. Overall, are you comfortable or tense? When you ask your inner self, the subconscious mind, how you feel about this—not what you think about it—what response do you get? Your body knows. If you'll listen, it will give you the right answer.

*Action step:* **Energy in action.** The next time you have a meeting, note where people sit in the room. You'll discover that, without fail, people tend to sit in the same positions every time. The VP will be as close to you as possible, while the general staff manager might always take the seat at the far end of the table. They're communicating with each other about pack hierarchy, allowing higher-ranking individuals to orbit close to the leader.

That's fine if you're just having the weekly go-around. But when you need the group to be responsive, creative and proactive, their self-generated seating chart will limit new ideas. The guy at the end of the table might speak only after everyone else, leaving little time for his ideas to be considered fully. The VP might dominate the conversation despite the fact that his ideas are the weakest. You won't receive the best your team has to offer, because their subconscious minds are utilizing the same old pattern that has taken them through weekly status meetings forever.

Whenever your team needs to generate new ideas, shake things up. Go into the room early enough to claim your seat—a new seat that's not at the head of the table. As each person arrives, greet him or her and gesture to a specific chair, a new chair for that person. If you really want to shake things up, put the VP in the general manager's place and seat the general manager at the head of the table!

Now, all heads will still turn toward you. You're still the leader. But now everyone is sitting across from someone different. The view they have of the room is different. You're asking their thoughts to be different, and you're communicating with their bodies by shifting the seating chart. Their bodies get it! Their minds will, too, the moment they walk in and see you in a new place. Something's up, something's new. They'll soon find out that their own minds are newer and fresher, and you'll reap the benefits.

*Action step:* **Change your words.** Profound change can come with the smallest of steps. In our daily conversations we often use the term "I want." When you express a desire and use this word, be aware of the implications. Want is to desire without having, so you've set yourself up to stay in a state of deficiency. I want a faster car equals you keep wanting a faster car. You can *want* all day long and never get it. Your subconscious mind, that stenographer who records everything in the most literal way, says "OK." The door of possibility is locked tight.

When you *choose*, however, you state your desire to have. "I choose to have a new car" means you choose to get it—and your subconscious mind says "OK." Now you are able to look for opportunities and action steps that will make your desire materialize. When you replace the word "want" with "choose," you open the door to creativity, to opportunities, to possibilities and to your imagination.

Let's say you choose a raise. Great. So, how much of a raise? Five hundred dollars? So you choose a five-hundred-dollar raise this year. No, every week! Oh, so specificity counts? How about 10 percent a year . . . compounding every year? Now figure out what it will take to create that raise: getting noticed! By whom? For what? Oh, man, I've got to be specific again? Yes! Now, do you choose to get the raise from *this* company? Oh, you mean I can go beyond my current situation?

Your mind opens up to possibilities and to questions. By searching your subconscious, your frontal lobe kicks in the creativity. When you imagine, you soar far beyond your current state of thinking.

Work with "want" versus "choose" and see what happens when you play the game full out. Teach your pack to choose, to ask questions, to open up their creativity and imagination. You'll be glad you did.

## PAWS FOR REFLECTION

*Dynamic cultures are based on*

*candid communication, creativity, adaptability and awareness.*

## CHEAT SHEET

# Remember Your Instincts

- We are energy. Everything around us is energy.

- What you think impacts your energy.

- Trust your intuition. Your body is responding to waves of energy and telling you something your mind needs to know.

- Since other people are also made up of energy, they will feel whatever you send out.

- Awareness of energy is a great start. Follow through by putting that energy into action. Remain aware of your thoughts, emotions and actions. Adjust your attitude to ensure you're producing the frequency that will generate optimal success.

- It takes only seconds to have an impact; the effects stick around for a long time.

- People constantly read each other's body language. They'll believe your body before they'll believe your words!

- Eliminate negative speech patterns and opposite answers. Speak your truth. Say what you mean. The words will focus your attention on your goals.

- Set the intention toward a positive goal. Generate possibilities without limits.

- Ask your subconscious mind how you feel about something. Your body will give you clues to the true answer.

- Shake people out of their old physical habits to generate new ways of thinking.

## CHEAT SHEET

- Replace the word "want" with the word "choose." Move from a constant state of being unfulfilled to an active journey toward your goals.

- Be specific! Your mind will generate exactly what you ask for. Implant the optimal goal for optimal results.

**Free tools at www.HowlLeadership.com**
*(Use VIP Code: ALPHA)*

# CHAPTER SIX

# Level Your Pack

In every wolf pack lives an alpha male and an alpha female. They are often called "the breeding pair" because they are the only ones to produce pups. If every female in a pack produced a litter, the wolves would soon decimate the stock of prey animals. The pack would die, and the ecosystem would fall out of balance.

To keep the balance, the alpha female has her own duties. She usually is the only female to produce offspring. She will continue to hunt with the pack during the two months of gestation. Near the end, she digs a den large enough for her and the litter of pups. As the pups grow older, the entire pack serves the litter through its different roles. The wolves watch for danger, bring down animals that feed everyone and play with the pups to help hone their skills.

When wolves move to a new territory, it's done under the watchful eye of the adults. The pup has time to get to know its new environment. The payoff is a tight-knit, cohesive, congruent and powerful force. Loyalty and trust are earned. Adults remain patient. Acceptable behaviors are demonstrated to the pups, and inappropriate behavior is corrected. The pups learn by watching and doing, by mimicking exactly what goes on around them.

All this effort is done for one reason: the pups are the future of the pack.

## Leaders Cultivate Their Packs

Now that you've done all the work laid out in the previous chapters, you know yourself much better. You are awake, aware and alive in the moment. You keep an eye on the future and your goals, knowing all the while that your past database provides you with important experiences that can be utilized by linear thinking. The Alpha Leader of your minds has nurtured and trained the subconscious and conscious for your own greatest good.

Now it's time to move from your private world to the public arena. You've set your inner wolf free with power, purpose and passion to generate spectacular results in your own life. To ensure that your company achieves its peak performance, you must do the same for every executive, manager and worker in your pack. You must train them in the same lessons.

Optimum success will be achieved only by taking this extra step. Since all businesses in today's high-tech, interconnected world are global, your competition is also the world. You need to build the loyalty and expertise of your team to stay ahead of the curve. By doing so, you will enjoy a clear edge over your competition. The time and patience needed to teach and train your own pups, your employees, pays off during the hunt.

As you build and demonstrate acceptable behaviors, values, skills and knowledge, you discover the immense talent hidden in each employee. You look beyond their résumés and their positions to find the innate skills and abilities they bring to your company. A community is built, and exuberance catches fire. You select leaders from the management and the skilled workforce. With subliminal, verbal and nonverbal training, the alphas of the future emerge.

You can have the best technology, procedures, equipment and knowledge, but it still takes people to make it all happen. Customers are drawn to people with passion, to cultures that cultivate honesty and to leaders who are adaptable. They look for the human factor. Call any office that gives you only a series of recorded messages, and you'll understand. Everyone likes to feel special, cared about and taken care of. Breed this into your leaders and your team, and customers will be drawn to you.

When you and your team operate inside an entrepreneurial culture, everyone is involved. Everyone knows their role and how their role generates success for the team. The results are that everyone buys into the bigger picture. Each remains an individual in terms of his or her talents and capabilities, yet all work cohesively. And there is always a "UDM," an ultimate decision maker—you.

Just as it only takes one drop of poison to taint a glass of water, your injection of inspired, creative and effective leadership can propel you and your team to ever-greater heights. With your new radical way of thinking, you cultivate the culture of your team, department, peers and company. You don't lead by committee, but you do recognize people as feeling, sentient beings. You apply the same skills you've used for your own success to that of your team.

Leaders should be allowed to grow at every level of the organization. They are the alphas and the betas within their own packs, the ones who can take some of the burden off your shoulders so you can focus on the entire team. When they are cultivated and allowed to flourish at every level, these dynamic individuals create a dynamic company. They are your pups. They are the future of your company.

**Train for Success**

When new peers or staff join your team, do you set them up to succeed? Being the new guy is tough. All the other employees know each other; they've already established ways to work with each other that are efficient and respectful. The new person doesn't have a clue who works best in what area. Starting a new position, even at the head of the pack, can feel like being dropped into hot grease.

Equally as important is how your pack feels about the new person. Someone new can stir up all sorts of feelings. The pack members don't know about his skills or abilities. They have a certain level of trust, but the new person still has to prove himself capable. And they don't know about his expectations, preferences or method of operation. Uncertainty creeps in at every level and into every interaction.

And how do *you* feel when someone new joins your established pack? Sure, you've vetted her. Human resources ran all the appropriate checks, and you've reviewed an impressive resumé. The interview went well or else she wouldn't be there. But the same uncertainties exist: she has to prove out, she has to gain your trust and confidence with her actions as time goes by. Until you're also comfortable, uncertainty impacts you.

In wolf packs, absorbing a new member is easy. The lone

wolf starts at the bottom of the hierarchy. By exerting his dominance and proving his abilities, he works up through the layers until he achieves his peak performance. Even when a leader is replaced by a beta wolf, the pack already knows that individual's skills, abilities and expectations. Since comfort, trust and understanding is built in, the takeover doesn't disrupt how the pack functions.

Humans are different. They can feel threatened, jealous, fearful, anxious, stressed or resentful of the new hire. These emotions generate negative energy that can impact the new hire's ability to succeed. Since the newcomer is unable to achieve peak performance, he or she can't serve the pack fully. Even when the new hire is successful, the pack might begin to break apart. No matter how much talent someone has, when he or she walks in the darkness of unfulfilled potential, it casts a shadow over the company.

People at any level can begin to shut down. They might become less productive or engage in petty gossip. Since they're always keeping an eye on the new guy, they aren't paying full attention to their own tasks. Productivity, quality and efficiency suffer. As the leader, you might get sucked into the black hole of having to listen to the complaints, empathetic yet unsure what to do.

You must manage these emotions—both yours and those of the pack. Be "straight up" from the beginning. First address your own thoughts and emotions. You have the tools to shift your thoughts, which in turn will shift your emotions. The mirror you're looking into must be clean. If you see a mask, a myth, a false facade staring back at you, go back and practice what you've learned.

It's a process. You're not expected to "get it" overnight. When you took your first steps in life and in business, you probably fell once or twice. But you kept getting up. Through practice, you started moving up the ladder of success. Soon you began running and jumping. This is no different. When you speak with your team, it's important for you to be honest, balanced and clear.

Give everyone permission to ask questions. Give the same permission to the new hire. My philosophy is that smart people ask a lot of questions because they're always trying to learn. If you receive an answer from me and you say you understand, I will hold you accountable. If you don't understand, ask again.

Asking again doesn't mean you're stupid. It only means I need to find a different doorway. My mind is very analytical. I operate with linear thought patterns that move directly from A to B to C. Someone else's mind might be creative or scientific or intuitive. My arrow-straight answer might lack the intuitive leap someone else needs for full understanding. If my answer isn't understood, I need to restructure how I present my thoughts so the other person's mind can make the leap.

I'm also a person who learns visually. A person who learns kinetically might need the picture described in active terms so they can imagine a tactile experience. Hearing an explanation might be insufficient for a person who learns best by reading. In these cases, I restate the answer and have it repeated in the other person's words until we're both satisfied that true understanding has been achieved.

Special note: If someone asks the same questions over and over during a prolonged period, it's time to find someone else to do the job. As a leader, you have to recognize when a pack member is sitting in the wrong place. Find the right person for that job and the right place for the other person.

## Monitor Growth

Now that everyone is working well together, you must ensure that everything moves forward as intended. With a good monitoring system, you can correct the course before something blows up. People are people, after all. Things might not go exactly as planned. Correct the learning and training as needed. It's much easier than fixing things after they've already gone wrong.

This is your time to ask questions. Bring the new hire in for a chat now and again. Make sure he knows the lines of communication are *really* open, that you're not just looking for a quick "Great!" before dismissing him. Ask specific questions: Is the project budget what he really needs to perform this duty? Are individuals on the team functioning well? Or, does he want to shuffle people around a little? What does he need that wasn't addressed in the beginning? And, what does his team need?

You're supporting a creative culture. With a creative culture, people often come up with new and better ways of evolving. Adapt by improving your thoughts and processes. Allow him to adapt by implementing changes in how the team thinks and performs. You can create a culture that encourages others to continuously upgrade. This creates an ongoing process that generates new ideas, better solutions, and greater success.

It's not always easy. Sometimes you'll have to take firm steps to get the point across once and for all. Early in my career, I received calls from subcontractors who were unable to get their calls returned by the project managers. The subcontractors were looking for answers, and the managers knew the subs wouldn't like what they could offer. If the subs called me, they always received an answer.

I grew tired of taking time out of my day to solve problems that weren't mine to solve. My project managers also had to learn they couldn't avoid unpleasant situations and push difficult calls off on me. When a question came in that wasn't mine to answer, I walked over to the project manager's office, pushed the speaker button on his phone, and began talking to the sub.

The project manager was forced to deal with the problem directly: no more hiding from the sub or pushing away the problem; no more endless voicemails left by increasingly frustrated contractors. Hanging out in limbo is a tough place to be. It also practically guarantees that future work by the same subcontractor will be less than sterling. They're also human, and humans resent giving great service for less-than-sterling support.

This is all about stepping into fear. Wolves will pass through their fear if the prize is big enough. Buffalo are large creatures capable of goring, kicking and stampeding the much smaller wolf. Yet they can be taken down by a pack that moves beyond the danger and focuses on the bounty of meat the animal can yield. The wolves understand that the opportunity is greater than their fear. Faith, courage and trust in themselves and in the pack override the negative emotions.

I took my project managers into the middle of the buffalo herd. With my guidance, the managers realized that the scary-looking problem wasn't so dangerous after all. Starvation, on the other hand, was a clear and persistent danger if they didn't take action. We needed those subcontractors, so we needed to address the problem head-on.

My firm steps allowed the individual managers to face their fears. When they achieved success, they realized that dealing with the issues was less painful than inaction. Avoidance creates anxiety. Every voicemail they received from those frustrated subcontractors added to their own stress, which distracted them from other tasks, which kept them from operating at peak performance. All this because they wouldn't return a simple phone call!

To *be* a leader takes more than a title. Entrepreneurial leadership, an approach that enables each member to become an entrepreneur in his or her job, is *feeling* leadership. It's about being aware of who you are and who your pack members are. Enthusiasm thrives, inventive people rise to the top and loyalty is earned. The culture is fun, effective, trusting and productive.

As word spreads, your organization becomes the company of choice. Top performers from all your competitors look to join your team. Top clients from every industry seek out your services. You are the catalyst, the trainer, the alpha who makes it all happen. You began within yourself and then applied those same lessons to your pack.

## Show Your Appreciation

Wolves strengthen their bonds through touch; leaders strengthen bonds with their people through touching words. Praise—sincere praise—is a huge part of communication. Pups and people proudly repeat behaviors that generate praise. You can also subliminally teach many people at once by praising one.

General platitudes aren't enough. You must be sincere, specific and direct. "Tom, thanks for a good job, buddy!" isn't going to cut it. No one really notices, because it's as common as being asked, "How are you?"

So let's eavesdrop on a different kind of praise: "Nancy, you really saved the day on the Wilson project. I felt completely confident when I went through our proposal. The amount of detail and the visuals you included sold the clients. Every page covered one aspect of the project—schedules, cash flow analysis, everything! Having it bound and using Wilson's logo on the cover made them feel like we know them. What a brilliant idea. I really appreciate your professionalism, timeliness and attention to detail. Thanks!"

*Now* Nancy feels noticed and appreciated! Everyone standing nearby also gets the message. They know exactly what impressed you about the presentation and precisely how each item benefited the company. Your peers understand what you did. They saw her proud smile and how enthusiastic she was when she returned to her duties. Without even making a conscious choice to do so, they will emulate it with their own people. Everybody wins.

Now, you don't have to roam the halls patting people on the back. You have a lot of options to ensure praise is given and received. If you want to thank a team, send an email to the whole group. Name specific individuals, and thank each one for his or her particular actions. By delineating what was done well, you set up tangible goals for future performance. Since people thrive on praise, they will strive to reach and exceed these levels with every new endeavor.

For groups or individuals, spotlight extraordinary achievements in the company newsletter. Include a photo so people in other departments will recognize that person. This generates cohesiveness in the pack even for staff who don't work directly with that person. Respect for the individual spreads, as does corporate pride. Since high performers are clearly receiving recognition, all the other employees double up on their own efforts with the hope that they will receive equal recognition.

One word of caution: Though everyone loves to be appreciated, not everyone likes to be noticed in a public forum. If someone will respond better with a personal thank you, honor who they are. To embarrass someone with public praise is the wrong move. For these folks, stop by their office in person, or give them a handwritten note. As always, be specific with your praise. They'll know it's genuine and will react with genuine pride and enthusiasm.

## Beyond Words

Promotions, stock options, bonus programs and raises are all typical rewards for sterling performance. You've heard it all before and likely already have a number of these rewards built into your company. But your employees have also heard of them before. These systems, while important, are so common they might even be expected.

The employees might feel they're being taken for granted and are not being fully appreciated. It's not that they're not appreciated—money is a tangible reward for tangible service. But to really bring the point home, you need to go beyond the standard operating system. You need to find solutions that ensure your peers and employees feel valued and respected in the months between raises and promotions.

Hosting a summer picnic, for example, is a less common way to reward employees. The holiday banquet is fine, but a picnic allows families to bring their children. Since the setting also is less formal, you'll enable people to learn things about each other they might not discover in the office or at a sit-down dinner. This bonding experience will reap rewards day by day as the pack members view each other in new ways.

You also don't have to make an enormous effort to communicate your appreciation. A gift card from Starbucks is a low-hassle, high-impact way to thank an individual. A leader who occasionally brings pastries in for the entire office or their team speaks volumes throughout the year. Order pizza or have a catering company bring in dessert to celebrate the end of a long project. The small benefits you provide for your pack reap large benefits in its performance.

All of these gestures create additional opportunities for the team to interact. The surprise factor generates positive talk at the watercooler. The enthusiasm spreads well past the individual or team who was rewarded, and everyone strives to achieve at least the same level of recognition. That's well worth the minimal cost for each gesture.

Wolves do the same thing. When they groom each other, they provide real-world benefits by removing parasites. Their contact also has a bonding component, relaying trust, respect and nurturing. They know they value and honor each other. When your pack members share a dozen pastries, they do so with honor and respect for everyone else gathered around the box. No one takes more than their share and everyone benefits.

### WOLF WAY #6: Create the Culture of Your Pack

Now that you understand the benefits of cultivating your pack, you need to take action. These action steps will provide a launching point for your own ideas. By generating a creative culture, you allow yourself and your pack to implement new ideas and opportunities. The benefits will be visible every day and at every level.

*Action step:* **Pack awareness.** Start with your conscious mind. Think about an individual with whom you've been having problems. For this hypothetical, let's say it's a man named Sam. The problem might be performance related, or it could simply be that he doesn't seem happy in his role. Pull his résumé from human resources and look again at his experience. Check off all of the things you know to be Sam's true strengths. Put an X beside items he's proven he doesn't do well.

Now pull his job description. Make the same notations on those pages: check marks for things he does well and X's for those he doesn't. Put the resumé and the job description side by side. How well does Sam appear to be suited to the job?

You might discover he wasn't a good choice at all. Since people are feeling, sentient beings with individual needs and goals, you might have a person who padded his résumé in order to get a desperately needed job. Perhaps the breakdown is with human resources, who needed to fill a slot and had only underqualified applicants to choose from. You might also have found that the interview process, in which people bond, didn't properly vet him.

This doesn't mean you have to fire him. Instead, consider how you might lead Sam toward peak job performance. Portions of the job he can't handle might be shifted to a more-qualified individual. Or, Sam might be underperforming because he is overqualified for that position; the weight of that knowledge breaks down his confidence in his ability to reach his chosen goals, which impacts his ability to succeed with any goal.

Then again, you might discover Sam is exceptionally well suited to the task. Consider how you might lead him to his peak performance. Think about every encounter you've had with him and all the things you've learned about him. Does he feel appreciated? Is he better off working with less supervision, or does he need more input to feel that he's part of the team?

Find a solution, and implement it. He will begin to achieve, to reach goals and to feel the pride that comes with success. Your company will benefit from his enthusiasm and hard work. Check in with him now and again to monitor the situation, and stay open to creative opportunities he suggests. Work with his subconscious and conscious minds, his thoughts and feelings, to generate optimal success.

*Action step:* **Creative rewards.** Now and again, sit and allow your mind to relax. Expand beyond the walls of your building, and imagine the surrounding region. What special things exist only in your community? There might be historical sites or a zoo nearby. Maybe it's a public hiking trail that's short and accessible. Once you have some ideas, consider an outing.

Yes, that's right … a field trip! Plan it for a Saturday morning, or shut down the office or department early on a Friday. Have tickets for the zoo waiting at the gate for anyone who signs up. Meet in the parking lot at the foot of the trail, and spend an hour wandering along the path. Suggest that specific employees pair off with someone they don't normally interact with.

Arrange for a guide to provide a behind-the-scenes tour for a small group at a historic site. The places don't have to have anything to do with your industry or the company. But the outings will be as effective as any high-priced team-building seminar you might send your managers to during the year.

Best of all, individuals from every level of your company can attend. Everyone will feel appreciated. Your unusual rewards will also send the message that your corporate culture is creative and innovative and that it takes advantage of new opportunities. The bonding experience will enhance job productivity.

If you're creative with your rewards, you won't have to spend much, if anything. Your bottom line will feel the impact, though. Your pack will pull together and hunt more effectively than ever.

*Action step:* **Integrate the new hire.** Hold a group meeting to announce the new hire. Enlist assistance in bringing him or her into the pack. Depending on how your company is set up, you might hold more than one meeting. You might even utilize a teleconference for satellite locations. This meeting is meant to speed up the long-term training, keep efficiency high, maintain quality control and minimize watercooler talk.

During this meeting, guard against falling into the old pattern of negative thoughts or feelings some people might express. Thoughts of what might go wrong and all the extra effort it takes to bring in someone new must be cut short. Instead, relay pertinent information about them: who they are, their background, when they're coming on board, their job responsibilities, who they'll report to. Then state what you imagine the benefits will be.

Be sure to implement the same response in your team. Ask, "What will be significantly better with Joe on our team? How can we effectively use his talents, past experience and ideas? How might each one of you help shorten his learning curve so we get the most benefit in the shortest amount of time?"

Focus everyone's energy, thoughts and emotions on the end results. Encourage them to buy in. Ask others to imagine how this new person can help the pack, other individuals and the company. Control the room. Write down what people suggest and who's willing to do what.

Be specific. Ask, "What does the first day, week and month of Joe's tenure look like?" Delegate specific actions to specific individuals. Match each person's unique skills and abilities to appropriate tasks. Set dates and accountability based on the conversation. You're setting the new hire up for success from the beginning. You're also setting up your company for peak performance with this new member.

Then congratulate your pack on their creative, constructive and congenial sharing. Let them know you appreciate them and their willingness to embrace Joe from day one. When the new guy starts, explain the plan and how each pack member shared in its development. When you introduce Joe to the team, mention which pack member came up with which idea.

These steps are all about praise. Praise is an important part of your role as a leader. It also conveys to the new hire everyone's enthusiasm about his arrival. It creates pride in each existing member's role in helping him integrate successfully with the pack. You set the example for how your pack can communicate better, how members can operate more effectively and how each new member is expected to be welcomed. And that makes everything much easier. Just like inside wolf packs.

## PAWS FOR REFLECTION

*Our world is not linear.*

*Our businesses and organizations are not linear.*

*We are not linear.*

*Long-term success depends on evolving strategies that come from dynamic individuals. Foster the leaders of tomorrow through creativity, adaptability and awareness.*

*Train the pups to be the alphas of the future.*

## CHEAT SHEET

# Level Your Pack

- Leaders cultivate their pack. For optimal success, you must train everyone in your company with the same lessons you've learned.

- Look beyond resumés and job descriptions to locate the best skills and abilities each individual can offer.

- Leaders should be allowed to grow at every level of the organization.

- Set up new hires to succeed. Make sure every team member knows why the new person is being brought on and what he or she can offer.

- Engage others' imaginations. Ask them to visualize how things will change once the new hire begins work.

- Monitor growth. Correct anything that's off course while letting the new hire know that communication, success and constant improvement are part of your corporate culture.

- Step into your fear. Help others step into their own fear.

- Show your appreciation through sincere praise. Be specific! The individual will feel genuine respect and others will know precisely what's expected for their own efforts.

- Be creative about rewards. Move beyond what's common and expected to generate a unique and meaningful experience.

## CHEAT SHEET

- Cultivate pack awareness. Know who your people are and where they fit in the hierarchy.
- Train your pups to be the alphas of the future.

**Free tools at www.HowlLeadership.com**
*(Use VIP Code: ALPHA)*

HOWL!

# CHAPTER SEVEN

# Avoid the Porcupines

Now nearly a year old, the pup has a few hunting techniques under her belt. She is intent on her own target. She first noticed the strange creature when she heard a rustling coming from the bushes. If she could bring it down herself, it would be quite a prize. She charges in—and runs snout-first into a wall of thorns. She backs up, yelping and swiping at the spines embedded in her lips and nose. The porcupine glances back only once as it leaves for a quieter location. The young wolf rubs her face on the ground, unsure what has happened but smart enough not to chase that strange creature.

Alerted by her cries, the rest of the pack appears and investigates the scene. The oldest wolves spot the porcupine right away. They circle it, and for a moment there is a standoff. Then the wolves lunge and snap from every direction. The creature spins, slapping its bristly tail at every mouth and paw. There doesn't seem to be a way to get past those spines.

Then the oldest wolf spots an opening. When the porcupine spins again, the wolf flips it over. That's it! The belly is covered only with soft fur. The animal squirms, trying to find its feet again. With a quick bite and a shake, the wolf finishes off the prey.

**No Time to Waste**

Wolves don't have a lot of time to waste. Arctic wolves, for example, live in one of the harshest environments on Earth. Their home is the tundra's glacier valleys, ice fields, shallow lakes and green flats. The temperature remains below zero most of the year, and the ground is always frozen. Since grass is sparse, arctic wolves often travel as much as eight hundred miles in search of musk ox and caribou.

Everything about wolves supports their lifestyle. Their coats are heavy and their senses keen. They live in packs to ensure they can bring down the large game. Lone wolves survive by eating lemmings and arctic hares. When new wolves enter their territory, they form new packs. Every moment of work, rest and play serves a purpose. It must if they're to survive.

As a leader, you also don't have time to waste. Everything about you and your pack must contribute to your goals. Your focus must be as intent as that of a wolf during the hunt. If you allow negative patterns to continue within yourself or your team, sadness and anxiety and lack of confidence will impact your bottom line. Your operations will be less efficient and less profitable.

Now that you've broken through the old negative patterns, you must ensure that new negative patterns aren't allowed to develop. Pay attention to your pack and the types of jobs you assign. Handing off a task that requires analytical thinking to someone whose personality is vivacious sets the person up for failure—he or she will be burdened with negative thoughts and emotions and a new negative pattern: *I'm a failure at my job.*

Hand that same person a task that requires energetic communication with others, and he or she will soar, with even more positive thoughts and feelings: *I am a success at my job.* The individual's attitude, enthusiasm and passion will grow exponentially. Every new task will be met with confidence and power. And since that team member is also sending out energy, others on the team will pick up on that power and confidence.

At times you might realize that, despite your best efforts, you've misallocated your resources. You assigned a task to someone who seemed to fit the role, yet that individual is struggling. *Don't waste time.* Correct the situation as soon as you can. Send in other pack members to show the young wolf what to do. If he or she gets it, great. Allow everyone to continue on their own road to success.

If the person doesn't get it, shift responsibilities. Although you might wonder what message that sends to the individual and the team, don't worry. As long as you let the staff member know you appreciate his or her contribution, the person probably will be relieved to be free of that burden.

No one likes to fail, and most people can see failure coming. When you shift duties to someone who's more capable and give the original person a task that's better suited to his or her abilities, you create success for everyone.

The project won't get bogged down in a substantial or unfinished task. The individual won't carry a negative emotional burden forward to future projects. The person's peers will appreciate the support given to their teammate, and they will know they too will be supported if they ever have trouble. The entire team will know their leader will work compassionately and efficiently to maximize performance, productivity and profitability.

Fast action equals fast results.

**Wolf Attitude**

Wolves kill for a reason: they need food. As they approach a herd of antelope, they don't become emotionally excited and massacre more animals than they need to fill their bellies. They economize their energy by targeting the weak, the old and the lame. And when they fail—and they fail quite often—they don't mope around thinking they're total losers because they missed a single antelope.

You must be like the wolf. Your hunt for profit, productivity and efficiency must never become personal. Some actions will generate the goals you set; others won't. Failure is not a personal burden to be carted around like an overstuffed briefcase. It's merely another data point in your information bank, a lesson that proves one way is not as effective as the other. Like the wolf, you must rest briefly and then try again.

Maintain the wolf attitude inside you. Remain unattached to personnel decisions, past failures and the potential that you might go hungry in the future. Act fully in the now. Utilize every pack member and every resource to create the most efficient plan. Choose to generate the best outcome from your current environment and you'll change your environment for the better. You'll keep climbing that upward slope to find better and better views.

I once worked with a woman who had achieved great success at a national firm. She was a sales manager, at the top of her game and the top of her field. Her position was stable; her income was high. She'd spent a lot of time planning for the launch of her own company. Her business acumen and her financial stability had made it all come together. She was about to step out into her own future, into her own success.

Yet she hesitated. When I began working with her, she claimed she was too worried about money to take the plunge. She feared that start-up costs, regular business expenses and the newness of her company would leave her with little or no income. The fear of future hunger had stifled her so much that she was at a standstill.

As we rummaged around her own "overstuffed briefcase," we located the real reason for her concerns. What she thought was anxiety over money turned out to be anxiety over her abilities. If she wasn't able to perform at the next level, how could she possibly create the financial support her new company would need? As long as she stayed in her current pack, with its existing support and other team members to pick up for her perceived failures, she didn't have to face her doubts—much easier to blame money.

We found a solution. She negotiated with her firm for a gradual transition. By easing out of her current position, she was able to incrementally tackle the learning curve required by her start-up. Her successes were, of course, balanced with a certain number of failures. But by maintaining the wolf attitude, by remaining unattached to the hunts that failed, she was able to keep going.

Her company took off, and she transitioned into a life of financial success and the freedom of owning her own company. She didn't allow anything to become negative; she refused to pick up new baggage along the way. By remaining unencumbered, she was able to travel the hundreds of miles she needed to successfully reach her prey. By acting fully in the moment, she let go of fears about future hunger and operated at her peak performance.

## Allocating Your Hierarchy

Every pack has a hierarchy. Wolves can change positions; the female who spends most of her life lower down can suddenly rise when she discovers her true purpose as a wet nurse to the new litter. By matching the skills and abilities of each person in your pack to specific tasks, you can allocate positions in your team's hierarchy for maximum results.

Now, this feeling style of leadership is in no way soft. You can't hand out tasks based on who wants what assignment. People are emotional beings, and so they might disregard their own skills to grab at something they're not qualified to do. A manager might volunteer for a high-profile project because he wants to advance in the company. A peer might want to bring in a multimillion-dollar contract because the coup would have a huge impact on corporate profits. But if those individuals aren't suited to the task, the failure will have an even greater impact.

You always remain in control. Know your people well enough to utilize their skills and passions to the fullest. Assign tasks so that you'll create a successful outcome, rather than only passing out titles and feeding individual self-satisfying desires. Align every project with a purpose, and align every individual to be able to understand his or her own contribution to the goal. The person might not get the high-profile position or the big contract, but he or she will achieve something more valuable: success for the individual and the entire pack.

Let's say you assign your star employee a certain duty. Although she's always come through for you in the past, suddenly her performance drops. She's making a lot of mistakes and isn't handling the pressure well. Although she has all the resources she needs to complete the task, something's gone wrong. After careful observation, you can't find any external cause.

You must know her well enough to realize that her learning curve is too steep. Perhaps her abilities simply can't expand fast enough to efficiently achieve this new level of performance. Help her by breaking the task into individual steps. Work with her to set realistic deadlines for each step; then check in between deadlines to monitor her progress. Even when things aren't going as planned, praise her effort. Make sure she knows you're there to help, even if you eventually have to bring in someone new.

Monitor your managers the same way. Know their personalities well enough to determine if they're driving their people too hard. A perfectionist (Sally, for example) who insists on doing everything her way is cutting off the creative flow that enables employees to find new and better ways of doing things.

Take Sally aside for a little mentoring. Show her that she can't always charge in on the porcupine; sometimes she must use a little finesse. Allow the entire pack to grow and flourish by experimenting. No, things won't always work out. But by supporting creative efforts at every level, you enable people to maximize their performance and keep people from adding new negative baggage.

Be sure the managers don't swing too far in the direction of becoming too soft. Feeling leadership doesn't mean everyone sits around and chats all day. Deadlines, accountability and schedules still apply. An employee who can't succeed at any task isn't suited to your corporation; cut them from the pack. Free yourself to find someone better, and free that individual to find their own purpose with a different firm.

You can also implement these lessons in your personal life. As a consultant, I once worked with an engineer for a major international corporation. He was frustrated and overwhelmed at work, and he was desperate for relief. No matter how hard he tried, though, he couldn't find any answers.

As we discussed his career, he revealed that his college years and job path had been dictated by his father. Math and science had been hammered into him as the only path to financial success and prestige. Yet he'd always wanted to be creative and artistic. His desire to please his father had pushed him into an education and a career that had nothing to do with his real skills, abilities or desires.

As an adult, he had this old story operating in full swing. He thought that to remain financially sound he had to stay in his current field. After all, he already had years of experience behind him. Taking off down a new path seemed foolish. But he was horribly unhappy. Worst of all, he knew he was sending those same signals to his son: *To be successful, you must be miserable.* What a terrible lesson!

He didn't want to train his pup that way. He also needed to find a solution that would maintain his financial stability while also providing an outlet for his artistic side. Fortunately, he had the power to choose. He imagined himself being happy at his job and created true satisfaction for himself in that arena. In his spare time, he took up art as a hobby, with an eye toward eventually selling some of his work.

After making the internal change, he spoke with his son. They talked about the young man's desires for his own future. The father made it absolutely clear that he'd support whatever his son decided to do in life. He changed the message he was sending so the boy could find his own greatest success. And, of course, he found the relief he so desperately needed in his own life.

Be proactive in your search to maximize your pack's performance. Get out of your office. Wander the halls and ask questions. People on the front lines often have the best view of the battle; you might be surprised by what you discover. You won't hear about these things if you don't ask. No one wants to be thought of as complaining or negative. They're not going to walk into your office and volunteer unpleasant information. You have to prove, by going on the prowl, that you truly are interested in solving problems.

When you talk to people about what's going well and what's not, be sure to ask enough questions to move past the symptoms. You might ask, "If you could change anything about your job/department, what would you change? Why? How would you implement the change? Who benefits most from this change?" Always thank them for their honesty.

Now consider the source of the problem. Is the issue really money, or is it a perceived lack of ability? Is the star employee breaking down under new pressure, or is she simply trying to do too much at once? Although your staff is on the front lines, only you have the overarching view of the entire company. Utilize the information each person gives you to trace back any issues to their roots.

Once you locate the real cause, take action. If appropriate, acknowledge whoever brought the issue to your attention. Implement new procedures, assign different resources or shift the hierarchy as needed. Only the wolf who hunts will ever take down prey. Only leaders who hunt for maximum efficiency will achieve peak performance in their peers, their staff and their company.

## Kill Excuses

Whether you're working internally on your own issues or externally on the pack, one of the biggest time wasters is excuses. This is different than taking time to discover why something went wrong. There are real causes for failure, and the reasons can take as many forms as there are reasons for success. You know you're hearing an excuse rather than an explanation when victim statements start to fly: *It's not my fault. I'm always busy. I don't have time to spare to consider my staff's performance.*

Uh, yeah. Here's what you're really saying: *I refuse to look at my own problems. It's easier to lay the blame elsewhere. My staff will stand or fall on their own.*

Now, *that's* a waste of time.

During the eight-month period when my Bell's palsy was readily apparent, I was the controller at a construction company. A woman interviewed for a position in the accounting department. Our exchange was professional, and I was very articulate. I remember this because speaking clearly was so difficult. I worked hard to make other people comfortable and to help them understand my words.

Afterward, the candidate asked the accounting manager if I was drunk. She saw the droop in my eye and face and made an assumption despite the detailed interview I'd performed. Now, I could have sunk into a "poor me" mode. Remember that I already was having negative experiences in public when I scared mothers and put off sales clerks. To have the same kind of assumptions impact my ability to perform at work could have been a devastating blow.

After a week of crying each night and living in an "Oh, poor me" mode, I had to use my mental acumen to get over myself and my situation. I started making jokes about my droopy face and my slurred words. That allowed my coworkers to lighten up. Even though I wasn't pleased with the Bell's palsy card I'd been dealt, it sent me on an internal treasure hunt. I had to look inside and find imaginative ways to interact with people. It was up to me to help them understand and become comfortable with my condition so we could function together at peak performance.

Another client of mine did sink into victim mode. She was a successful businesswoman and wife. By outward measures, she had it all. Yet she never felt happy. She constantly found herself feeling anxious and often started arguments when there was no real reason to do so. There was no joy in her work or her life, and she needed answers.

As we talked, she remembered playing outside one day when she was around seven. She was with her friends and having a great time. Then her parents called her inside. Her grandfather, with whom she'd had a close and loving relationship, had passed away.

Her experience was similar to my own when my brother Steve died. I'd been having fun, anticipating my parent's arrival and the holiday festivities. When the bad news hit, I spent years living out my story: if I ever would dare to have fun, bad things would happen. My client had registered the same type of information in her own database. She was so terrified of being happy that she actively picked fights whenever joy threatened.

Although she never said or thought *poor me*, she was trapped in a victim mentality. Her grandfather's death had felt so overwhelming she became locked into a fear of future tragedy. Although death is a natural part of life, her inability as a seven-year-old to understand the event and to separate it from what she'd been doing before hearing the news caused lifelong anxiety—a fear of being happy.

Her anger was the clue. Since feeling like a victim is a very powerless place to be, she tried to take back her power by making other people victims. Her old story caused her to sabotage any feelings of happiness in herself. She also sabotaged the same feelings in everyone around her. Both were symptoms of the real cause. Once she worked through the original event, she imagined herself happy. She became comfortable and secure in her own happiness.

Wolves never make excuses. They don't point to a fellow pack member as the source of their own trouble. They don't blame the weather or the terrain for their failure to bring down prey. They simply move on, utilizing the best of what's available to them in the moment. They take proactive measures and travel those long distances to find prey. They feel hunger and experience failure, yes. They also keep searching, maintaining the cohesiveness of the pack by allowing themselves to try again.

Kill your own excuses. Kill excuses in others by moving past the symptoms and addressing the cause. Work in the now with an eye toward the future. Maintain your stability while always striving to bring down bigger prey and achieve better results. Choose to free yourself and your pack of any burdens. Move forward with a wolf attitude for optimal success.

## WOLF WAY #7: Engage Your Wolflike Focus

Everything you do must move you, your team and your company toward its goals. Just because we've talked a lot about emotions doesn't mean action isn't important. Benchmarks, timelines and accountability are still important with this feeling approach to leadership. Put guidelines in place, and you'll assure the success of your pack and your company.

*Action Step:* **Align every project with a purpose.** We all love our PowerPoint presentations. The steps of a project are laid out along with timelines and individual assignments. But how many presentations actually lay out the purpose of the project?

To reach your goals, you must keep them in sight. Your entire team must know the specific, concrete results you want to see at the conclusion of every project. Delineating them ensures that every individual is aware of and striving toward your expectations.

As always, be specific. The conclusion of a contract obviously brings more money into the company. Yet there are many other benefits that accrue, and each one should be noted as a measure of success. Taking on a larger project than usual enables the company to seek equivalent contracts with other clients in the future. Assigning new responsibilities stretches your team beyond their current capacity and adds to their abilities. Working with new clients expands your network of referrals.

Outlining the goals also expands your team's vision. They see what's possible for the current project and how success can generate future opportunities. Their passion is stirred because they can see beyond their current duties. They know their efforts will pan out in ways far beyond the milestones of the current project.

You also let them see your own vision of success. When that image becomes their own, everyone is focused on the same result. Everyone pulls together. Time, energy, effort and resources automatically fall into place. You don't waste a single minute, a single dollar or a single team member.

*Action Step:* **Align every individual with a goal.** Here you're implementing your hierarchy. Just as every step in a project has an individual trajectory that culminates with the end result, each team member has their own path that will merge with others' paths during the project. You must know each individual's path, and that person must see it as clearly as you do.

First, ditch the organizational chart. It's too vague and doesn't delineate specific tasks. Instead, set up a timeline and results chart. At the very top, write the overall results this team as a whole is going to accomplish. Let's assume your overall result is "Customer XYZ Signs the Contract." Down the far left side of the chart, list the names of the individual team members. Then run a timeline across the bottom. Depending on the project, it could be charted out in hours, days, weeks, or longer—whatever is appropriate for this particular project. Down the far right side of the chart and directly in alignment with each team member's name, write their specific purpose for being on this project. For example, Tim's purpose is to "provide clear, concise financial data to ensure the customer feels secure about its investment." Sharon's purpose is to "create a vivid detailed picture of why your company is the best choice, so that the customer understands the value of working with your company." Randy's purpose is to "gather all pertinent information on the customer, which will be included in the proposal, so the customer knows it's understood and cared about." You get the idea. Every team member has input into this process.

Now, each member states what they will do and by when, to accomplish their portion of the project. Chart these notes and dates horizontally along the timeline across from each person's name. Discuss overlaps, ensuring that two people are not doing the same task. And discuss gaps, to ensure no steps are left out. Also, if a member needs data

## Customer XYZ Signs Our Contract!

| RESPONSIBLE | ACCOMPLISHMENT | ACCOMPLISHMENT | ACCOMPLISHMENT | END RESULT | How? |
|---|---|---|---|---|---|
| **Tim** | Description of what Tim will complete in this time frame. | Description of what Tim will complete in this time frame. | Description of what Tim will complete in this time frame. | Ensure XYZ Co. feels secure in their investment. | Provide clear, concise financial data. |
| **Sharon** | Description of what Sharon will complete in this time frame. | Description of what Sharon will complete in this time frame. | Description of what Sharon will complete in this time frame. | XYZ Co. knows we're the best choice. | Create vivid, detailed pix of us. |
| **Randy** | Description of what Randy will complete in this time franre. | Description of what Randy will complete in this time frame. | Description of what Randy will complete in this time frame. | XYZ Co. knows we understand and care about them. | Include pertinent information on XYZ Co. in proposal |
| | **Date/Hour Due** | **Date/Hour Due** | **Date/Hour Due** | **Completion Date/Hour** | **Project Review Date/Hour** |

from another member to finish their portion of the project, build this into the timeline. It requires an agreement by both members and is best agreed to upfront.

Now you have a plan, a goal, a purpose and results. Everyone on the team has bought in. At the end of the project, celebrate your accomplishment of working together and completing the project on time. Also, meet as a team to discuss what worked well and what areas may need to be tweaked for the success of future projects. Create an atmosphere for open, honest communication and improvement.

Several people might follow up with clients to ensure they were satisfied or to ask for referrals. Certain individuals might develop new skills as part of their goals. Include yourself on this chart along with your own pathway. The team will know you're still at their center and that you'll continue to be proactive with this project.

The entire team should clearly see that they are all responsible for the largest goals: coming in on time, controlling costs and generating a quality product or service. By blending the individual goals and the overarching goals, you create the expectation that everyone will work together for everyone's greatest good.

*Action Step:* **Schedule feedback.** Build into the timeline opportunities for the group and individuals to provide feedback. Right before a milestone, you're likely to hear about what's going wrong. Immediately after a milestone, you're likely to hear about what went right. You'll also gain the benefit of your team members' hindsight. They'll be able to look back at the problem and see things they couldn't in the heat of the moment.

Be sure that everyone feels free to offer advice and new ideas at any time. By scheduling feedback, you prove that this is possible … and expected. As the leader, you should always be the first to hear bad news. Don't allow negative thoughts and rumors to circulate through the entire company before someone finally works up the courage to tell you.

Never shoot the messenger! Although the problem might send you rocketing into the stratosphere, stay calm when the news is delivered. Otherwise the messenger will think you're angry with them. You'll be much less likely to hear about new problems later if everyone's afraid to speak up.

Thank the person who brought you the problem, even if that person is the source of the problem—especially if he or she is the source! It takes courage to deliver the bad news, and you want to hear it. If you don't know about problems, you can't fix them before they sink the entire project.

## PAWS FOR REFLECTION

*Maximize energy and minimize time.*

*The more people you have on the field,
the fewer people you have on the bench.*

## CHEAT SHEET
# Avoid the Porcupines

- Don't waste time. Everything about your pack must contribute to the goal.

- Prevent new negative patterns from developing.

- If you discover that you have incorrectly assigned a project, take action immediately. Fast action equals fast results.

- Your hunt for profit, productivity and efficiency must never become personal. Maintain a wolf's attitude and remain unattached to personnel decisions, past failures and potential starvation.

- Allocate your hierarchy. Match the skills and abilities of each person to specific tasks for maximum results.

- Feeling leadership is not soft leadership. Deadlines, accountability and schedules still apply.

- Be proactive in finding problems. Ask enough questions to move past the symptoms and locate the real cause.

- Kill excuses. Eliminate victim statements. Constantly move forward for optimal success.

- Align every project with a purpose.

- Align every individual with a goal.

- Build into the timeline group and individual opportunities to provide feedback.

- Never shoot the messenger! You need to hear the bad news so you can eliminate the problem and avoid even more bad news down the road.

# Express Your Power

The Navajo called on the power of the wolf's spirit during healing ceremonies. Their word for wolf, *maicho*, actually means "witch"; it was thought that by donning a wolf hide, the wearer could transform himself. The Cheyenne rubbed their arrowheads against a wolf's fur so they could bring down animals to feed their tribe. Successful Mandan warriors tied wolf tails to their moccasins as trophies. When the northern lights danced in the sky, the Cree believed divine wolves were visiting the earth.

This deep respect springs from the wolf's power. It also reflects a careful observation of the wolf pack in its natural environment. Hunters wanted to emulate the wolf's prowess, while warriors strove for wolflike bravery and skill. The wolf's focus on the pack as a whole inspired healing ceremonies, and the pack's nurturing of the young was a good standard against which to measure human interaction.

Modern people can take the same lessons from these ancient animals. Even today when a wolf pack lies down to rest, the alpha pair is always at the center. Their every movement draws attention from other members. Their body language and vocalizations tell the pack whether to react to danger or rest peacefully. Their pups, the future of the pack, are also watched closely to ensure their safety. The leader is accessible, central, visible and dominant … without being domineering.

## The Myth of Fear

Other cultures had their own myths about wolves. In Europe, the fear and dread surrounding these powerful creatures produced tales such as *Little Red Riding Hood*. These powerful predators were thought to kill sheep and, whenever possible, humans. The fear was so strong it was thought the gaze of a wolf could cause blindness; a horse that stepped in a wolf's track could go lame; and the breath of a single wolf was hot enough to cook meat. The hysteria was so widespread that naturalists of the day thought wolves sharpened their teeth before hunting.

When Europeans arrived in America, they brought this crippling fear with them. They immediately tried to destroy the wolf population in their new home. High bounties were paid for wolf skins. In some colonies, the rewards were so high they drained all the town's funds. The prize generated corruption when individuals presented the same wolf head several times to claim several bounties. When only the wolf's ears had to be proffered, people used fox or dog ears.

The excessive level of control the settlers tried to implement on their new surroundings bankrupted a lot of towns. It also generated unnecessary fear for the welfare of livestock and humans. Because the settlers' lack of understanding extended to other parts of their new ecology, they rapidly depleted the wolves' game and forced them to attack livestock. This "proof" of the dangers generated more fear, higher bounties and more corruption while depleting resources that might have served other needs.

The same cycle threatens your wolf pack. Leaders who rely on excessive control and fear tactics are working with false systems. They implement corporate myths that disregard the natural way people and systems operate. Micromanaging every task drives out the star performers you need for peak performance. Inflexible, domineering leadership destroys the creativity that might enhance operations. It also destroys the passion that could set your profit margins on fire.

True power is not about excessive control or instilling fear. True power is based on respect and understanding, the interchange of different ideas and the merging of different skills in a group. This loops back to the idea about leveling: every individual is a leader at his or her own position. All actions by every individual are for the good of the group, the department, the company.

It all begins with you. You are always at the center of your pack. You must remain accessible, visible and dominant without becoming domineering. You must respect the skills and talents of every member of your pack to help them achieve peak performance. They, in turn, will respect you. The stories that spring from these interactions will reflect power, wisdom, peace and strength.

The same respect will flow to those outside the pack. Your clients, sister companies and contractors will know they are respected for their own roles. They will know their own talents are valued, and they will achieve project goals because they respect your company. Their own passion will fuel ever-greater results as your relationship with them grows.

Before it can begin with you, it must begin inside you. The Arikara tribe tells of a time when the earth was covered with water. The face of the water was empty except for a few ducks. As Wolf and Lucky-man looked down from the sky, they imagined a very different kind of world.

This new world would have space for many different kinds of creatures. Dry land would spread out into plains and mountains and valleys. There would be plenty of room for everything, and everything would have its own place. The ducks dove deep under the water to bring up mud for Wolf and Lucky-man to build this new world. Soon the prairie bloomed and the hills rolled from horizon to horizon.

As powerful as Wolf and Lucky-man were, they couldn't create the large creatures. They were humble enough to know that large creatures could only be produced by the growth of the smaller ones. They called on two spiders to help. The pair created more eight-legged creatures like themselves. The six-legged insects followed, and then came the four-legged animals. Finally the two-legged animals, the most powerful creatures of all, were born.

You must be like the sky wolf. You must recognize that your own power grows out of creatures with different skills. You must be humble enough to allow every person at every level of your company to do what he or she does best, to function at the individual's own peak performance. You have the originating vision to create a new kind of environment for your company. You set the stage; you create the wide prairies on which the pack hunts new clients and you create the fertile valleys of base camp. Then you must step back and allow the pack members to do their jobs.

**Power is Not Force**

The colonialists tried to bring sheer force to bear on the wolf. They rallied individuals from all walks of life by offering rich bounties. Humans outnumbered wolves from the start, so it seemed like a good plan. But since humans were intimidated by the wolf's power, their hysteria was driven by pure emotion. They lost any logical concept of how the lack of funding for future initiatives might impact their survival. They were caught up in the emotional impact of myths they'd brought with them from the motherland.

Aggression and intimidation are forceful measures. They instill fear, anxiety and stress. They turn a capable, functional pack into a hysterical mob. Leaders who rule with domineering, intimidating measures distract their employees from the company's goals. If everyone's constantly ducking down to avoid the latest fire from the head office, if they're constantly worried about whether they will displease the big boss, how much work is really getting done?

Power is sometimes mistaken for yelling the loudest or slamming a fist on a desk. These actions create fear, and fear does not yield power. Fear is created by force. Force is aggression, a way of pushing people around. If you mistake force for power, your team will operate with fear-based reactions. The fight-or-flight response will always muddle the operations.

You might get away with it for a while but the consequences are stress—for you and everyone in your space. People shut down. No one's thinking clearly. Clarity, production, effectiveness and quality go out the window. There is no benefit to force.

Authority, on the other hand, is the legal power to enforce. Police officers and governments have authority. Your board, the owner and the corporate officers have authority. Company policies and procedures list the principles you have the authority to enforce.

And then there is power. You might claim the fancy title, the biggest office, the highest paycheck and the closest parking space. But power is the capacity to grant or withhold cooperation. If you give orders and your team members don't respond, they hold the power. Your team has the power to cooperate … or not.

Oh, they'll *look* like they're cooperating. They'll nod their heads and scurry off to complete the tasks you've given them. They'll jump when you enter the room and do whatever's necessary to please you at that moment. The second you leave, though, they'll sigh with relief. They'll do *only* what's necessary to meet the deadline and not a bit more. They'll follow those procedures and rules no matter how ineffective and inefficient they are. They'll do it because they want to keep their jobs, not because they want the pack to achieve its peak performance.

Consider this simple scenario: One employee consistently arrives five to ten minutes late every day. Although no one else seems to care, your window looks out over his parking spot. You know exactly when he arrives every morning, and you are counting up the hours lost every month, every year. You chew him out and then start meeting him at the door every morning, checking your watch in a not-so-subtle way.

What you failed to observe was that this same employee stays late *every* night, and not just by five or ten minutes. The extra half hour or so of work he put in—and what those numbers added up to every month, every year—went uncounted. Maybe his morning tardiness was a direct result of staying late because he couldn't take care of all his personal obligations in the evenings. Since you've forced him to arrive on time every morning, he has to cut out the extra time spent at work every night.

He also doesn't *want* to stay late anymore. His passion has been extinguished because you didn't respect the extra time he put in. He now goes by the book—in by precisely 8:00 a.m. and out at precisely 5:00 p.m. You failed to understand the full ecology of this worker's movements and didn't respect the contribution that was above and beyond what was expected.

Not anymore! Now he's ticking off a mental checklist meant to keep *you* happy, a checklist that has nothing to do with keeping the company healthy. He's choosing to cooperate within the strict boundaries your force laid out. He had the power to work late before; he maintains that power by cooperating only with exactly what you ask. Your fear that the company was losing money to consistent tardiness resulted in inflexible, domineering action. His response is fear based and resentful.

Force is not power. True power is based in respect and humility. Allow yourself and your company to grow by respecting the contribution of every two-legged creature in your ecosystem. When you respect others, they will respect you. They will choose to follow you. They will choose to perform at their own peak level for the good of themselves, their teams and the company.

## Leadership Is about Energy

An alpha wolf, the pack leader, can be male or female. The alpha wolf isn't always the largest wolf in the pack, but he or she does head up the hierarchy. The complex social order is never static. Wolves can move up or slip down at any time. The dominant wolf is obeyed, and his authority and decisions are generally respected. Often, the better he is as a leader, the friendlier and more serene his relationships are with other members. The pack leader's power is based on decisive self-confidence. Loyalty and trust are earned.

The alpha doesn't stalk around biting other members whenever it's time to hunt. He simply stands up and trots off, knowing the pack will fall in behind. A powerful leader doesn't gain strength by making people do something. Real power comes from within. It has a vibration. It comes from truth and inner strength, from expressing genuine feelings and from self-knowledge. When you truly know yourself, everyone gets it. They naturally fall in because they get *you*.

When you know yourself, you can influence others—not manipulate but influence. To wield influence is much more powerful, respected and effective than wielding force. People choose to follow you. They are *happy* to follow you. They admire you and want to please you by doing a great job. Their loyalty expands.

I once coached a financial advisor. He felt burdened by his daily routine and by his life in general. As we worked together, he realized that he pictured himself like Atlas: bent over carrying the world on his shoulders. This subconscious picture impacted everything he did. No matter what happened, everything took superhuman effort, and it showed.

Once he imagined himself free of the world's burdens, he filled the void with a new image. He generated a picture of himself standing tall, unburdened by issues that weren't his to solve. His body responded by shedding the burden of his excess weight. His professional and personal life improved, and he began to thrive.

By changing his subconscious image of himself, he set the intent for the rest of his life. He didn't have to carry that overwhelming weight, either mentally or physically. Freed from that burden, he was able to stand tall and generate big changes. Although he hadn't meant to influence others, everyone around him noticed the change. His intention had been picked up by others, and he attracted a new love relationship.

Whenever you prepare for a meeting, take a moment to set your intent. Know that you are capable and strong, and that your power will work for the benefit of all. Take action based on this knowledge. Sit at the head of the table when you need the full focus of your team. Alternatively, sit somewhere else when you need others to take the lead on specific projects. If you really want to shake things up, don't even sit at the table; push your chair against the wall and let the group have at it!

You can even implement powerful actions on an individual basis. Rather than calling someone into your office, plan to meet in their office. Give them the home turf advantage. Let them sit behind their desk while you sit in front; or, remove the desk out of the equation entirely by asking them to sit in a spare chair across from yours. These nonverbal signals open individuals to deeper levels of communication.

If you want to maintain a little formality, bring a clipboard. It provides a slight barrier yet also enhances their feeling of being respected when you jot down some of their ideas. It also creates expectations—you've made a note of something, so they know you'll expect that idea to be implemented.

As a leader, it's important to know when to use your power and when it's best to stay in the shadows. Practice humility. Observe. Learn from the verbal and nonverbal language of every individual as he or she interacts with you and others. You'll gain much more than you would if you always run the show. Step back so that new leaders can emerge and the company can prosper.

Now, hierarchy still exists. There always needs to be that ultimate decision maker, the UDM. Yet today's employees won't tolerate military-style management. For better results, encourage entrepreneurial leadership within your company. Level out the organizational chart. Real growth occurs when you recognize and rejoice in the vast knowledge and skills of your workforce. Real growth occurs when you utilize these resources to their full extent.

Create a flexible and changing hierarchy in your pack. Allow others to take the UDM position on different projects. They are your beta wolves. Each will take on a different leadership role; each will take responsibility for a specific area. You'll still be at the center, visible and accessible, able to provide advice and guidance as needed. You'll also be free of the minutia they're handling. Your ability to generate new visions for your world will expand, and you'll work at your own peak performance for the benefit of the pack.

It begins, and ends, with you.

## Lead by Example

When people want to follow your lead, they begin to emulate you. They copy your attitude and your approach to problems. They work hard to understand how their own tasks will help their team and the company. They want to see things the way you do, to apply your principles to how they operate. When that happens, you are well on your way to creating The Spirit of Entrepreneurial Leadership™ within your company.

When necessary, take action. If someone or something threatens the fabric of the pack, the leader responds immediately. Protect and defend your pack as a whole. A person who is disruptive, who holds values that are different than the pack, who isn't pulling their weight or who growls at other members—that person must be dealt with swiftly.

This applies even if the person is your best producer. Whatever that person does to undermine the efficiency and effectiveness of the whole cannot be tolerated. Just as one negative, nagging, sabotaging thought can shut down the genius of your mind, one poisonous coworker can kill the genius of your pack. Take appropriate action, even if it means saying " Buh-bye."

Assertively communicate your ideas. Be inspirational. Share a common vision with clarity and passion. Lay out the road map of how you and your pack will achieve the goal. People need to know where they're headed and how to get there. Their conscious, linear minds feel at ease. When that happens, they can engage their subconscious, creative, intuitive minds for new and better ways to achieve the end result.

Lead by example. Teach your pack members to take risks. Not every project will pan out, but if their ideas come out winners most of the time, it adds to the bottom line. Status quo is not growth. The best professionals work off averages, and they don't quit when they're off their game. Instead, they go back to the basics and figure out what to do next.

As a leader, you must do the same. Say what you mean, and mean what you say. You can be a great orator, but if your actions don't back up your words, the pack will believe your actions. Remain alert to what you say and what you do. If they don't match, figure out why and then fix it. You must be in alignment; your energy must match your language, in order to be effective.

## WOLF WAY #8: Cultivate a Cohesive Pack

True leadership is created when followers choose to fall in behind. The alpha respects each pack member for his or her unique skills, and the members respect the leader's confidence. Because it starts inside you and then comes from you, these action steps work both internally and externally.

*Action Step:* **Use your instincts.** Humans tend to shut down their instincts, even their five senses, when they make decisions. It's important to integrate the left-brain process of gathering and analyzing information with guidance from the intuitive, subconscious side.

After gathering and analyzing information on your next project, do a gut check. Is your body in turmoil? If so, it's disrupting your energy flow. Something's not right. It's going to impact you. You will not be projecting the confident, capable leader you choose to be. Your team will immediately pick up on your shift of energy in your demeanor and your behaviors.

Follow the disruption through to its source, using the same visualization techniques laid out in previous chapters. Once you've located the source and imagined a new solution, engage your conscious mind again to take action on the solution. You'll be able to move forward with confidence in your own decisions. Your pack will naturally fall in behind with complete faith and respect for your abilities.

*Action Step:* **Stay rooted in your own energy.** As a leader, you must always stand solidly on the foundation of your own positive energy. You can't afford to buy into someone else's panic, anger or anxiety. That can be a difficult order; since emotions are energy, you naturally pick up those vibrations. The trick is to be aware of the energy others send out and to utilize your own calm, decisive flow to restore balance.

I once took a call from a subcontractor who was extremely angry. As a general contractor, we couldn't pay the subs until we were paid by the project's owner. Our clients' payments were late, so our payments were late. By the time the sub talked to me, he was in full attack mode. He was angry over the delay, fearful we would never settle and probably anxious over whether he could pay his own bills.

After listening to his ranting for some time, I started saying his name. No matter what he yelled, I repeated his name over and over. When he finally said, *"What?"* I asked him to do me a favor. Again he hollered, *"What?"*

"This weekend," I said calmly, "drive up South Mountain. Get out of your truck, sit on a rock, cross your legs and hum for fifteen minutes. On Monday, when you're calm and more relaxed, call me. I'll update you on payment then. I know you want your money. The minute I get it, you'll be the first on the list."

There was a pause and then . . . laughter. "Damn you," he said. "You know I'm just looking to get paid."

From that moment on, we were best buddies. I had refused to buy into his energy, to become as angry and fearful as he clearly was. By maintaining my peaceful, calm, commanding attitude, I shifted his energy. He learned to trust and respect me. And yes, he did get paid first!

*Action Step:* **Teach others the same lessons.** When I was a COO and a partner in my construction business, I taught my VPs and managers the same lessons I had applied to myself. Every Friday morning, we met to discuss different aspects of these techniques and to share how implementing them had panned out. The first two weeks were mandatory. After that, they kept coming because they got so much out of the sessions.

I used my personal library of books and audiotapes in the sessions. Titles like Ayn Rand's *Atlas Shrugged* opened discussions on how underappreciated workers could destroy companies by "going on strike" and refusing to contribute their peak performance.

You might prefer to use historical examples. African American slaves and concentration camp workers both utilized work slowdown methods to confound their masters. They were oppressed, enslaved and tortured, yet they maintained power in a way no whip or gun could destroy.

No matter what your approach, these sessions will yield benefits far beyond the time involved. In my company, our discussions expanded our minds. By reading or listening to books the VPs and managers typically wouldn't have picked up otherwise, they increased their database. Talking about both what they liked and didn't like about the new information sparked lively discussions. We took away from these meetings new perspectives, new information and new ideas. For a small investment of time, we reaped great rewards.

## PAWS FOR REFLECTION

*Right now, right where you are, begin creating your new history.*

*Accept that you are capable and successful.*

*Engage that confidence every moment of the day.*

*You'll naturally become the leader people choose to follow.*

*You'll naturally achieve true power.*

## CHEAT SHEET

# Express Your Power

- Leaders who rely on excessive control and fear work with false systems.

- Micromanaging drives away star performers. Domineering leadership destroys creativity.

- Remain accessible, visible and dominant without becoming domineering.

- Respect the skills and talents of every pack member.

- Stay humble. Know that your success grows from the success of your peers and everyone working at all levels around you.

- Force is not power. Aggression and intimidation instill fear, anxiety and stress.

- Power is the capacity to grant or withhold cooperation. Your team has the power to cooperate . . . or not. True power is based on respect and humility.

- When others choose to follow you, they choose to perform at their peak for their own good and the good of the company.

- Create a flexible and changing hierarchy to allow others to take leadership roles. Your work will become lighter, and your beta wolves will grow in their own right.

- Lead by example. When you have true power, your team wants to emulate your attitude and your approach. Your goals become theirs.

- Back up your words with actions. Teach others the lessons and attitude you know works best. Allow

## CHEAT SHEET

them to integrate it in their own way for their own optimal success.

- Stay rooted in your own energy. Lead others to reflect your calm, capable demeanor for everyone's best benefit.

**Free tools at www.HowlLeadership.com**
*(Use VIP Code: ALPHA)*

# Bond With Your Pack

Wolf and Cougar have always been enemies. They hunt the same prey; they live in the same territory; and they sometimes kill each other's young. There is no love between them. Sometimes they even kill each other.

One day, Wolf was out alone. He was hoping to start up his own pack but hadn't found any other wolves to team up with yet. He found plenty of small game but missed the taste of deer. Whenever he found deer bones, he gnawed them just to enjoy their flavor.

One day he came across the bones of a cougar hidden in the tall grass. What a treat! He hardly ever had the chance to gnaw the bones of his enemy. He settled down and soon lost himself in this immensely satisfying activity.

Far up on a ridge, Crow had watched Wolf wander his new territory for some time. Crow was a real clown and liked nothing more than stirring up trouble. When he saw Wolf settle down, he thought he'd tell Cougar about this interloper. He quietly flew off and found Cougar napping on a rock. Soon he led the big cat back to where Wolf was busy with his unusual snack.

This was the perfect time to strike. Creeping through the tall grass, the big cat drew very close to his enemy. Wolf didn't notice until his attacker was close enough to pounce. He had to think fast. Although a lone cougar was no match for a pack, a single wolf faced real danger.

Then he got an idea. He stopped gnawing the bone and looked across the plains. Licking his lips, he said, "Gosh, that cougar sure tasted good. But I'm still hungry. I wonder where I can find another tasty cougar to eat."

Cougar froze. He began to panic. Obviously he had underestimated this particular wolf! One cougar was already dead; he might be next on the menu! With his fur puffed, he backed away as quietly as he'd crept in. The wolf listened closely for every movement. When it was finally safe, he loped away. Sitting on the top of a nearby ridge, he laughed and howled with Crow. The joke was on Cougar!

**Play for Profit**

Wolf pups love to play. They are curious about their world and explore everything. They stalk each other, pounce on the adults, growl and wrestle and romp. For them, everything is new and wonderful. A bone or a feather becomes a toy to be chewed, tugged and carried around like a trophy. When something new enters their environment, they watch it as closely as the adults.

All these actions have a purpose. The pups really are practicing the skills they'll need to survive later on. They learn what they can do, as well as their limits. They exercise their muscles and mimic what others do. Since less-aggressive animals get less food at feeding time, the hierarchy of the new generation develops early in life.

By the time they are six months old, they begin hunting with the pack. At first they hunt small animals like rabbits. Through additional training with the adults, they gradually learn how to take down larger prey. Their practice as pups enables them to quickly become productive members that contribute to the pack.

When the day's work is done, the entire pack howls. Although howling is used to gather members together before a hunt and to warn other packs away from their territory, apparently it's also done just for fun. Rather than howling the same note, each member adds its unique voice to the music. Even the pups join in. Howling is yet another way the pack enhances its unity … and what a sound!

Play is efficient. Yes, that's right—play is efficient! Having fun releases stress. The emotional components of joy and laughter create a stress-releasing chemical cascade through the brain-body feedback loop. It generates a relaxation response in the physical body and mental state, which frees us to move forward with a fresh perspective and new energy.

Laughter really is good medicine. It reduces chronic stress, increases lifespan, boosts the immune system, protects the nervous system and gives your endocrine system (in the fight-or-flight mode) a much-needed rest. The physical action of laughing moves fluids through the lymph system, oxygenates the blood and boosts circulation. The brain produces serotonin, which relieves depression and boosts immune-system chemicals such as interleukins. If you tried to purchase all the chemicals produced by laughter from a laboratory, it would cost roughly $10,000.

Having fun also does much more. Just like wolf pups sort out the hierarchy early on through their rough-and-tumble games, play helps people bond. When we're at play, the formal bonds that might keep us from smiling much at each other are put aside. We laugh and joke and enjoy each other's happiness. We add our own unique voices to the game. We howl!

Now, all of this might sound fine. And, you think, there is the company picnic and the corporate banquet. Plenty of play going on there … sort of, anyway. Good food, lots of chitchat and maybe a little dancing or a ball game. Well, wolves don't wait for the semiannual lupine ball to reap those benefits. They play every day. They howl nearly every night. They benefit from the same relaxation response, the same bonding that people enjoy when they do the same.

Of course, no company can set aside time to play every day, at least on a formal level. But you can, and should, allow for frequent playful interaction among your pack members. Some of the world's leading companies started with a foundation of creative freedom. By experiencing joy while at work, employees bring creativity to their jobs. By being more relaxed, people are able to focus fully on their tasks. Productivity, vision and passion propelled these companies into the industry leaders they are today.

Play is an incredibly powerful tool. Savvy leaders know this and implement play into their corporate cultures. They utilize the pathways of joy and fun to open the subconscious minds of their pack. Some of the activities work as training sessions to enhance interaction and skills. Others are simply fun—they allow the pack to bond in the strongest way, by sharing laughter and joy.

### Workplace or a Working Family?

In a previous chapter, we discussed rewards: salaries, promotions, stock options and other common incentives. We also looked at less common rewards that can achieve even greater results: field trips and weekend hikes, for example. But tangible rewards aren't the only things feeling beings need to achieve true satisfaction. To really pump up your team, try playing with the pack.

We can see the results in how wolves interact outside their species. A research group that raised wolves from pups tried an experiment. The researcher placed a piece of meat in a cage where it was visible but not accessible to an adult dog raised separately by the team. After a few minutes of trying to reach the treat, the dog sat down. It looked from the human to the meat and back, clearly asking for help. Under the dog's watchful eye, the researcher opened the cage and gave the meat to the dog. The adult wolves had a very different reaction. Long after the dog had given up, the wolf continued to scratch and bite at the cage. It never stopped, and it never looked to its human caretaker for assistance. Although it had been "tamed" by its upbringing, when the researcher tried to intervene, the wolf growled and snapped. Although it couldn't reach the meat, it also wasn't willing to share with any creature outside its species.

Yet in a natural situation, the same wolf would share the kill with its pack. The hierarchy still exists, of course, and higher-ranking animals will consume the greater amount of the reward. Still, every pack member receives some portion of the kill. This sharing with its own family group ensures the survival of the pack.

Your company can't afford to have pack members view each other as outsiders. They must work together to achieve rewards, and the results must be shared out according to your pack's hierarchy. When you implement measures that enhance the bonds within your entire company, you ensure the survival of your pack.

Note that even during play, competition is healthy. While operating my construction company, I encountered other business owners who knew this. Kristine, an innovative accounting assistant, started assigning gold stars to project managers who approved and returned their invoices back to accounting in a timely manner. On a bulletin board in the lunch area, the project manager who was the fastest (while accurate) received three gold stars, the second received two and the third received one.

Since there was no financial reward attached to the gold stars, it was clearly a game. Yet the results were that each project manager worked hard every month to see how many gold stars could be posted next to their names. A lot of joking went on in the company because of it, which meant people outside that department also participated in the fun. The return on the investment in a twenty-nine cent pack of stickers enhanced more than the bottom line.

I've seen the same results in individuals I've coached. One woman was ready to make a change in her life. She was held back by something, yet she didn't know what that something was. When we worked together, she remembered that her parents had often made comments whenever she'd tried something new. "Are you sure you can do that?" they'd ask. "That's a really hard thing to do. Don't be disappointed if it doesn't work out."

Now, they were trying to support their daughter. They always said that no matter what happened they would always love her. But that's not what she heard. Her perception of herself and her abilities sank. *I'm not good enough*, she thought. *I can't do it. It's too hard.* She carried this subconscious programming into adulthood. When faced with a change she truly wanted that presented challenges, she was held back by thoughts of inadequacy.

The thing about play is that it circumvents this type of programming. There are no negative consequences attached to a game. No one's going to lose a job or a big contract, and everyone has fun. Yet play is often challenging, and competition arises in a healthy way. By succeeding at play, people learn they are more capable than they'd thought. They rise to a challenge with passion and inspiration. They recognize they can do hard things … and that doing hard things can be fun!

Play has a place at work. By allowing employees to have fun, you enhance their bonds. The naturally competitive nature of individuals comes out in a healthy, pleasurable way. It costs little or nothing to implement games here and there, yet the results are measurable. Play creates a family in the workplace. The pack that howls together hunts together!

## Playing Well with Others

In addition to having your pack members bond with each other, they also must play well with others. Your team can't view outsiders—other departments, other companies or clients—as a different species unworthy of rewards. You must ensure that your staff moves beyond any notion of boundaries. Their focus must be on peak performance for the benefit of all. By generating rewards that everyone shares, your pack will rise to the top of your industry.

It's easy enough to implement play within a single department or company. After all, you're in control of your territory. Using the same approach outside your company or department might be a little more difficult. So bring the same creativity and vision to these efforts as you do to your own projects. Move beyond what's traditional and expected. Access your subconscious mind and see what happens.

I have firsthand experience in this area. My construction company sat on a lot directly across from one of our suppliers. We sometimes talked, but we didn't really know each other; we were corporate neighbors. Our sales manager decided we should occasionally play together. Our games went way beyond a sack race at a community picnic. We had water fights!

Once in a while, we'd give the receptionist her marching orders—no filing, no typing that day. Her only duties were to answer the phone and fill balloon after balloon with water. The rest of the staff continued working but occasionally sent faxes over to the neighboring company. *Prepare yourselves, they read. Surrender now and save yourselves. Prepare to be annihilated!!*

The other company sent faxes in return. *You're toast,* they read. *Watch your back!* I can just imagine them scrambling to prepare their own ammunition. Anticipation grew as the box of water balloons filled up. At the appointed time, both companies' employees poured out of the buildings. We charged the street dividing our lots and lobbed balloons back and forth. Shrieking, war cries and laughter ensued.

As our sporadic battles continued, we got a little more creative. Those huge toy guns that shoot streams of water became part of our arsenal. We both built slings to shoot our water balloons farther. One time we brought in a water truck. When the other company charged out with their pathetic little balloons and big toy guns, we drove the water truck down the street and soaked everything and everybody.

One day, the joke was on both of our companies. Our screaming and war cries were so enthusiastic someone from another company called the police; and they responded in force, expecting to quell a riot. They even sent a helicopter!

We had a lot of explaining to do that day. But it all turned out well. The officers were clearly amused. They weren't "our species," yet they had shared in the pleasure and passion that rewarded our companies.

**Genuine Fun**

Play can't be forced. No number of special events can generate true pleasure if that same energy doesn't come from the leader every day. You must exude real enthusiasm, real pleasure whenever you interact with your pack. Remember, this is all about you. It starts with you and within you. You are the center of the pack during all serious times; you must also be at the center during the fun times.

Join in. Don't just set up a fun activity and then stay in your office working while others try to have fun. Remember, they'll believe your body language, your actions, before they'll believe your words. They might participate because they think you expect them to, not because they think they'll actually derive pleasure from the activities. Use the opportunities you create for them to bond with each other and as an opportunity so they can bond with you, too.

When wolves howl, they do so with the leader. They might participate at different levels, but every pack member adds a unique voice to the mix. You might not compete with them for gold stars, but you certainly can acknowledge their pleasurable competition. Yes, praise them for having fun! This attitude will extend to everything they do. They'll feel respected and will know that their every action receives your attention. They'll work hard every day because they want to. They receive a bonus, as does your company.

I once worked with a successful business owner who felt something was missing from her life. She worked hard and was very passionate about her career, yet she wasn't truly happy. During our sessions, we discovered that when she'd been a child, she'd had the same passion toward all of life. She was creative and loved to have fun.

Her mother was a strong, kind woman. She raised her daughter well, teaching her many of her own habits and attitudes. However, she never praised her daughter's creativity or encouraged her to have fun. This generated mixed feelings. The girl knew she enjoyed being creative, but there was never any positive reinforcement for those things. The leader in her life didn't participate in or encourage fun activities.

Her automatic patterns were shaped by her mother's reactions. She grew up knowing how to be strong and work hard. But without imagination, her life had become blocked. She gave herself permission to have fun. She relaxed, and her creativity soared. She reconnected with friends and found that everyone began commenting on how creative and innovative she was. They also praised her for being a fun person to have around!

As a leader, when you implement fun at the workplace, you're building new automatic patterns with your team. You're utilizing the brain-body chemical feedback cascade to reinforce pleasure. You're allowing everyone to feel relaxed and connected—to you, to each other and to other packs— every day they come to work.

Best of all, you're replacing the old feeling of discomfort, anxiety and nervousness people naturally feel toward strangers and authority figures with a bond. Since people won't be distracted by that tension, they'll bring their full mental game to their projects. They will operate at peak performance individually and within their teams. They will also derive more pleasure from everything they do, which will enhance the well-being of your company.

A different client of mine had survived cancer. She was a brilliant woman, charismatic and enthusiastic about many things. Yet she didn't see those traits within herself. She certainly didn't know how strong those traits were. Since she believed herself to be unworthy, two important areas of her life were giving her less than she deserved. She was in a poor intimate relationship and had a poor financial condition to match.

She clung to her beliefs that she was not worthy. She'd already had parts of her body removed to address the cancer; she wasn't about to allow anything else to be removed. Once she realized this, she was able to let go of her old beliefs. She ended the relationship and began moving up in the world financially. Because she generated those changes within herself, changes in her external world naturally followed. She found a man who inspired her, one who appreciated the intelligent, attractive person she really is.

The attitude within affects the attitude without. As a leader, you must cultivate the attitude of passion, enthusiasm and true joy within yourself. People will respond to your energy. Your employees will emulate you, and clients will want to work with you. When you draw these new people into your corporate life, your career and your company will soar. Every aspect of your life will feed into your continued success. Every success will feed into the success and joy of your pack.

A wolf's howl can travel as much as six miles. Your howl can travel even farther than that. Let it loose! Exploit the natural state of humans: understand that we are all emotional, feeling beings. Harmonize with the other voices. Generate the bonds that will carry your pack through good times and bad. Celebrate every triumph; celebrate every day. Allow the echoes to create greater joy and prosperity for you, your pack and your company.

## WOLF WAY #9: Plan for Pleasure

Police officers and soldiers have long been known for battlefield humor, making jokes when faced with the most horrific scenarios humans can suffer. Even when your corporate battlefield looks grim, you can—you should—integrate play. You'll relieve everyone's stress and anxiety, enable them to change their perspectives, and harness the brain-body chemical feedback loop in a way that will generate powerful change.

*Action Step:* **Laugh.** Oh, boy. Tall order, right? The sense of humor is notoriously individualistic. The Three Stooges will make one person double over in laughter and another person double over with nausea. That's all right. In this action step, you're only focused on making yourself laugh.

You know what you like. Make time in your schedule to do things that make you laugh. Watch a funny movie when you go home at night. Take your kids to the water park … or go with your adult friends! Eat lunch at a place where you have to use your fingers. Whatever makes you laugh, do it!

*Action Step:* **Play at work.** Schedule a meeting. Don't say what the topic is but tell them it's a planning session. When they arrive, break out the finger paint. Ask, "What do you want?" and have them paint a picture of their goals. Leave the topic nonspecific. Some people will paint personal goals, while others will stick with their careers. The most inspired of the lot will recognize that the two intermesh and will paint both.

A less messy option is to plunk a stack of magazines on the table. Make sure to mix publications of all types—business and travel magazines, fashion and celebrity publications, real estate and pet catalogues. Everyone gets a pair of scissors, a glue stick and a large piece of paper. Tell them to create their treasure maps.

At the center or to one side, they will glue a picture that represents where they are right now. Spiraling out from this will be pictures that represent the milestones they expect to achieve during their journey. They might have a single goal or several; their goals might interlock or be unrelated. It's their map!

Although they might feel a little silly at first, silly is good … it's fun! Be sure to sit down with them and create your own image. Pay attention to what's going on in the room. I guarantee you that within ten minutes everyone will be relaxed. Soon laughter will follow.

An added benefit to this game is how their minds process the task. Their subconscious, intuitive minds generate a pictorial image that represents a goal. Their conscious, linear thoughts organize those images into a comprehensive flow on the page. Not everyone can do this focused kind of mental work solely in their heads, so this physical task allows them to practice integrating their two minds.

For both the finger painting and cutting-and-pasting exercises, leave a few minutes at the end for sharing. You'll find that the images everyone created are as visually unique as the people in the room. Some will paste their pictures into neat rows; others will paint splashy images that flow intuitively. Your team will bond during the experience and by sharing their goals, visions and dreams.

Plus, since everyone's picture will be equally messy, no one has to worry about winning or losing!

*Action Step:* **Play well with others.** Make sure your team doesn't view anyone as an outsider. You want to keep boundaries from being drawn between departments internally and other companies externally. Even your clients have a role to play; make sure they're considered part of the global pack.

Plan a handful of events throughout the year. Have human resources randomly match people from different departments for a "secret Santa" exchange. Make sure the employees have enough time to skulk around and find out what the recipient might like.

Have all the presents turned in to HR before the Christmas party. As individuals arrive at the party, they can pick up their gift. Everyone opens their present at the same time; then the secret Santas go around and talk face-to-face with the person who got the gift. They have fun for weeks ahead of time; they anticipate the big reveal; and they get to know someone they otherwise might never have met. They bond with the other packs inside the company in a fun, playful way.

Bonding with sister companies or subcontractors or clients doesn't have to be a big, coordinated effort. In the middle of summer, ask for volunteers to participate in a beach party giveaway. Let them choose from different gifts: a beach towel, a plastic bucket and shovel, a packet of seashells.

Then have them handwrite a note on company letterhead about why they selected that gift. Bundle everything up and send it over to the other company. Let that company distribute the gifts as they like. The goodwill, and the surprise of receiving a personalized gift, will enhance your relations for the rest of the year. And when clients refer you to someone else, you can be sure they'll mention that fun gift!

## PAWS FOR REFLECTION

*Enhance the fun factor in your workplace for peak performance.*

*Howl!*

## CHEAT SHEET

# Bond with Your Pack

- Play is efficient. Having fun releases stress and induces the relaxation response in the physical body and the mental state.

- Play allows people to bond in new ways and on new levels.

- Play utilizes the brain-body chemical feedback loop for positive results.

- Through joy and laughter, the subconscious mind opens. A new perspective is brought to the workplace to enhance and improve operations.

- Make sure no one is an outsider. Other teams, departments, sister companies and clients must all be viewed as the same species.

- Competition is healthy. The fun competition that arises during play impacts the bottom line. Everyone strives for new levels.

- Play circumvents the negative thoughts created by past events. Since no one's keeping score, there isn't any worry over whether an effort will be good enough. Play teaches us we really do have a lot of skills and abilities!

- Be creative in how you implement play into the workplace.

- Join in the fun. Howl with your pack!

**Free tools at www.HowlLeadership.com**
*(Use VIP Code: ALPHA)*

# CHAPTER TEN

# The Wolf's-Eye View

When a wolf pack grows too large, individual members split off to find new territories. Usually this happens during the fall, when most wild animals are dispersing over wider territories to forage for scarce food. Often the wolves that leave are younger than three. They are old enough to have learned everything the pack can teach them and young enough to have the energy needed to forge their own path. Eventually they meet up with other lone wolves and establish a new pack.

Even when wolf packs are stable, there are times when the alpha splits off to be alone. He or she goes to a ridge to look out over the territory. From this vantage point, the alpha can locate any threat and monitor the movement of prey animals. When they return with this new information, they can better lead the pack into the future.

## Inspired by the Lone Wolf

I stood transfixed as tears ran down my cheeks. Before me was a simple yet powerful painting. A solitary gray alpha wolf stood proudly atop a bluff. His ears were erect and his tail curled high over his back. Below him, pups played their war games and some of the elders slept. Others surveyed the land spread out around them, their territory.

I was attending a leadership group in Jackson Hole, Wyoming. The group had been asked to wander around the seminar hall or even venture out into the crisp air of the Grand Teton Mountains until we'd found something to which we felt connected. I never made it out the door. The psychologist who led the group gently set his hand on my shoulder.

"What do you see?" he asked. "What is it about this painting that makes you feel connected?"

"That's me!" My tears streamed faster than I could wipe them away. I pointed to the solitary wolf. "I'm the one who looks out for everyone else. I'm constantly ensuring that everyone is OK, that no unseen danger lurks in the forest. I can come down to play, to teach and to hunt. But my role is to always look out for the greatest good of the pack."

There weren't enough tissues in the building to keep up with my tears. I caught my breath and blurted, "It's sometimes very lonely up there, but it's where I've chosen to be."

The key word is chosen. We must all be comfortable in our own skin. In choosing to have our own voice and our own dreams, in taking responsibility for our decisions and our mistakes, and by accepting the chaos that comes with new opportunities, we breathe the breath of freedom. You know how to do this now; you've learned the lessons of the previous chapters so well that they've integrated themselves into your subconscious programming.

You've also learned the importance of teaching others those same lessons. Like the lone wolf, leaders must rejoin the pack at times to lead the hunt, to teach new lessons and to keep the pack functioning. You must utilize the same lessons you've applied to your internal and external worlds, your conscious and subconscious minds, in behalf of your entire company. By doing so, you'll leverage strength and energy to create leaders and passion at every level.

## The Spirit of Entrepreneurial Leadership™

Organizations all over the world are recognizing that even with the highest level of technology and precisely defined procedures, they are still not working at maximum efficiency or reaching their desired profit margins. It's because of their people!

The greatest variable between you and your competition is the environment or culture in which your organization operates. That culture is made up of people. The most volatile part of your business is your people. Your management team needs to be proficient at leading those people.

The days of inflexible managerial hierarchy have given way to leadership at every level. Lots of managers fill the halls of today's corporate world, but few leaders stand among them. Managers are tactical. They ensure that timelines and objectives are met. They are obsessed with details, details, details. But where have all the leaders gone?

We need people who are self-aware, confident, realistic, idealistic and motivating. Employees look to leaders to make decisions and then back up those decisions with confidence and dedication, with actions that support the decisions in meaningful ways. Leaders aren't afraid to make a mistake. They emanate a presence wherever they go. You can feel the energy change when a leader enters the room.

Along with leaders, we need a new culture for today's organizations. People don't take orders very well these days. They don't want to feel as if they're in the military. They don't want to follow commands on blind faith. They demand the right to know why. And that's great, if you understand how to gain the confidence and enthusiasm of your people to benefit them and the organization.

Old-school thinking has given way to The Spirit of Entrepreneurial Leadership™. Each part of this new approach connects with and supports the others. First is spirit. Spirit is a connection between the mind and the emotions. It is the essential nature of a person or organization. Spirit is passionate and purposeful. Spirit has real sense and real significance.

An organization that is entrepreneurial feeds into spirit. An entrepreneurial company is self-directed and creative. Importantly, it has the ability to apply that creativity. It is comprised of risk takers who strive to create value through the combined efforts of its people and the organization's structure.

Leadership is the ability to influence and gain commitment from others. This is accomplished through authentic behaviors and attitudes applied to a predetermined set of core values and goals. The leader demonstrates interpersonal and intrapersonal knowledge. He applies that knowledge with compassion, courage, vision and fairness.

Many good books about leadership have been written by highly intelligent people. However, simply reading a book won't make anyone into a true leader. You must make a personal commitment to understand what is necessary to change a culture. You must accept the need for change and believe change can occur. Then you must incorporate values and beliefs, vision and goals, purpose and passion in the organization.

## Feeling Leadership

People are emotional beings. They are not computers or machines; they harbor their own unique stories, histories and experiences. They are truly your greatest resource. They are the one resource whose performance can be enhanced by bringing creativity and flexibility into daily operations. They are the only resource that can improve the bottom line through passion and enthusiasm. You do not have to change out their parts every year; and through your consistent guidance, they will never grow obsolete.

Feelings have a place at work. You can't eliminate them, so why not utilize them? Every judgment and decision, although seemingly implemented primarily by logic, is processed through the emotional side of the brain. The brain-body chemical feedback loop can turn anxiety into anticipation, fear into courage. Awareness of these hidden processes and actions that free their power creates loyalty and efficiency in your pack.

I once received an email about a group of students who were asked to list the Seven Wonders of the World. After some time during which the students worked individually, the teacher tallied the answers. The usual items showed up on the list: Egypt's great pyramids, the Taj Mahal, St. Peter's Basilica and the Grand Canyon were among the offerings.

But one student struggled to complete her list. When the teacher asked that individual to share what she'd written, she said, "The Seven Wonders of the World are to see, to hear, to touch, to taste, to feel, to laugh and to love."

The room was so quiet that you could have heard a pin drop.

It's amazing, really, that we overlook and take for granted the simple and ordinary things in life … things that are truly wondrous! The most precious things in life can't be built by hand or bought by man. So, what makes hearts skip a beat? What is it that would make the world perfect for you right now? It's not the past. It's the thoughts most leaders would describe as taboo, soft, inappropriate for the business world and certainly not in a leader's vocabulary.

But in today's world, a leader is expected to be more human, more compassionate and more real. I'm not proposing soft leadership, but feeling leadership—authentic leadership. Understand who you are so you can truly understand why you behave the way you do. What are your drivers, your hot buttons? What sends you into your office with your head spinning and your heart palpitating in fear?

More importantly, *why?* Once you determine why you behave in a certain way, you can make a decision to release yourself from your past. You can make a conscious decision to live in the now. During the process, you'll also identify what makes you want to get up in the morning and come to work.

There is a whole lot more to being a leader today than setting a strategic plan, giving directions and solving day-to-day issues. You also need to be in tune and in touch. Your attitude and behaviors will set the tone for everyone else. Take care that the message is enthusiastic, purposeful, and supportive of your goals and the path to them.

Purpose and passion work together. With purpose comes passion. With passion comes a burning desire to succeed. When passion and purpose are aligned, anything is possible. When the company has a clearly stated common purpose, employees move forward with confidence. They feel the freedom to be creative. A collaboration grows when everyone believes The Spirit of Entrepreneurial Leadership™ truly exists. Everyone works together to strategically and tactically plan for success.

Everyone feels much more passionate because they see themselves as contributors to the greater vision. They have purpose. Whether the goal is to improve a task, a procedure, a department or the organization is of no consequence. It's not the size of the project, the urgency or the project's importance that matters. People need to be needed. They need to be appreciated and valued. They need to belong.

No matter how big or small the project, it's important to clearly state the purpose, the vision and the deadlines for each benchmark. It's also imperative to select the appropriate team members for each task. Lines of accountability must be established and monitored. Everyone must understand that open communication is imperative. As a newly evolved leader, you must meet the basic needs of your people. Then your pack will jump to make any project a success.

## The Creative Corporate Culture

There's a new breed of employee out there today. They want or, more accurately, they expect their lives to be balanced between work and personal time. They still want to work hard, have goals, be ambitious and succeed. They also want to work with *intention*. They want to know the answer to the all-important question, "Why?" Somewhere along the way, they lost the why. They want it back. They need it back!

As a new leader, it's up to you to answer that question. To do so, you first must examine the human side. People are born to be creative, to produce, to be adventurous and to succeed. That hasn't changed. All human beings are equipped with a brain, a heart, feelings and the need to have purpose attached to everything they do. Yet the corporate world has fenced people into cubicles, given them tasks and said, "Do a good job. Your paycheck depends on it."

As children we asked, "Why?" Though it sometimes became a bit annoying to our parents, our inquisitive minds were constantly fed answers. Our parents bragged to their friends how smart we were for asking so many questions. Our excitement, curiosity and creativity soared. A gentle pat on the head gave us the approval we so desired. Our inquisitive minds were happy and so were we. All was good.

Asking why generates a response. Responses generate knowledge. Knowledge generates more questions. Often in today's work culture, leaders fail to give enthusiastic and purposeful questions the necessary attention. We often demonstrate by our behavior that questions are a nuisance and have little value. Workers have become conditioned to not ask why. They follow procedures and policies; they check off completed tasks. This is supposed to equate to a successful day.

Yet, at the end of this supposedly successful day, the employees feel unhappy and unfulfilled. They leave work dreading the next day and wake up dreading going to work. But they need that paycheck, so the cycle continues.

As a leader, you might have lost creative and ambitious employees when the organization didn't exude an entrepreneurial environment. The employee eventually became tired of being put in a box and so sought out an organization that embraced his or her creative nature. Other employees learned to bend and concluded it was best to squelch their creativity. In both cases, the organization suffered. It will never fully benefit from the untapped resources of an employee's intelligence, dedication, creativity or passion.

When new employees are hired, the saga continues. They are quick to note how other employees are treated. They soon figure out how they should behave to ensure their jobs remain stable. This type of culture makes employees frustrated and unwilling to take creative risks, and it kills motivation. Everybody loses.

This culture begins when leaders discuss organizational needs. They determine strategic goals, assign projects to appropriate managers and then pass directions downstream. Frequently members of the leadership team are at odds even before a project begins. The differences aren't discussed, and they remain unresolved. Strategic goals don't clearly fit into the organization's vision and purpose. This is the beginning of the breakdown.

Pressures are passed down the food chain. If luck is on their side, everyone will know what is expected and when it is expected. The problem is that no one knows why. They are not privy to the bigger picture, the vision for the project. They are left wondering how their participation will make a difference. They simply add the task to their list, check it off and then go back to their daily routine. They never see the effect of their contribution or how it has impacted the bigger picture. Passion doesn't exist. Creativity is never encouraged.

Why should I put my priorities on the back burner for this important project? What is our shared vision? Why must I contact an owner to notify them of their overpayment? Is my staff willing to go the extra mile? Why does this important decision seem right but not *feel* right? Do I need to explain a project in detail to my accounting manager when my sales manager just wants the bottom line?

How different it will feel when everyone is aware of the common goal. When properly focused, the project team has vision, purpose and intention. Every eye will be fixed on the desired end product. Each team member will be committed to success. People will fully utilize their heads when their hearts have been fed.

The Spirit of Entrepreneurial Leadership™ has specific objectives: values and beliefs, vision and goals, purpose and passion. To achieve these, you must understand yourself, your people and your peers. While this is not an easy set of objectives, it is essential for true success—that means organizational success, interpersonal success and intrapersonal success. Trust me, the journey will be both enjoyable and awakening!

As a leader, you must become fully aligned with both intention and attention. You must set your intention on what you want to accomplish and then apply your full attention toward achieving it. This is authenticity.

Authenticity enables creativity. It frees the best of every employee at every level of the organization. They don't need upgrading because they constantly upgrade themselves, their procedures and their performance. Passion drives them to higher levels of success. They become leaders by applying their own unique experiences and databases in positive, powerful ways. They bring new ideas to different projects and to their daily operations. They enhance, streamline, implement—and produce.

All because you applied the best of your leadership skills to their departments, their teams and their positions. All because you enabled their creativity to come into the mix. All because you allowed leadership abilities to flourish at every level.

All because you answered their why.

## It Begins with You

What's your vision statement? Where do you see yourself in one year, three years, twenty years? Some managers say, "I just want to keep doing the very best I can at what I'm currently doing." Now there's a statement that inspires you to get out of bed every morning … not!

Today's manager needs to be at the cutting edge of The Spirit of Entrepreneurial Leadership™. They must lead, level and leverage their pack. To accomplish this, he or she must know him or herself extremely well. If you go home at night feeling unfulfilled and burnt out, consider yourself flatlined. You're merely existing, not living. You can't inspire others if you're not inspired.

Once you fully understand how your life experiences have molded you into the person you are today, you'll better understand everyone around you. People might have been created equal but our life experiences generate a wide degree of variance in how people respond and behave.

The Silent Generation survived World War II and the stock market crash. They are loyal to their employers, who provide them a paycheck in return for hard work. They believe in structure and its enforcement. Then came the Baby Boomers, hard-working, success-driven people who produced latchkey children and suffered high divorce rates.

Now those latchkey children are becoming the leaders of tomorrow. Generation X wants a balance between work and pleasure. They experienced the results of two-income families, and they don't want their own kids to miss out on having parents around. They are also very adaptable and insist on working with the latest technology. Though highly educated and intelligent, they are inexperienced and cynical.

They want everything now!

The workforce also contains both men and women. Women are no longer limited to receptionist, secretarial and accounting roles. They are now effective senior executives and owners. The "Old-Boys' Club" has faded. Women are more detailed and compassionate, as well as great problem solvers and decision makers. Knowing how the genders mix at all levels of business and how they might communicate more effectively is as important as blending the different generations within your company.

People all over the world—male or female, young or old, rich or poor—all have feelings. What makes them happy, proud, sad, fulfilled, scared or excited is different for each one. That's the beauty of our differences. We are feeling creatures, and leaders need to acknowledge this and then create a culture that allows our most desired feelings to be met.

Now we've gone full circle. We are back to the need for The Spirit of Entrepreneurial Leadership™. As the army recruiters say, "Be all that you can be." This must hold true for everyone in the organization. Everyone must be authentic to themselves and to the organization's values, vision, culture and intention. By creating a culture that enables this freedom, employees become purposeful and passionate.

Encourage people and their breakthrough thinking. Be willing to reward success . . . and even reward intelligent failure. When people think outside the box, they won't succeed every time. Michael Jordan didn't make every basket, but his spirit was strong enough to keep him trying.

Wolves don't make a kill on every hunt, but they don't just give up and die. Sometimes you have to take risks, break rules and go against the status quo. Sometimes you fail. Failure is an event. It doesn't define the individual.

# WOLF WAY #10: Live an Entrepreneurial Life

You've learned a lot in this book about being the Alpha Leader of your minds. Now that you've trained yourself and everyone around you, there's one more step you can take. Adding authenticity and The Spirit of Entrepreneurial Leadership™ will supercharge everything you've done and everything you've become. Use these action steps as a launching point to generate results that are even more powerful.

*Action Step:* **A wolf is a wolf is a wolf.** Authenticity is about being who you are. It's about the little things as well as the big issues. Get rid of pretense. You don't need smoke and mirrors to make your magic; when your energy comes from being fully aware of who you are, it will naturally conjure everything you want.

Pick one thing you feel obligated to do. Stop doing it. Don't wear a tie five days a week. Pick flats instead of those painful pumps. Sell that horrific, heavy oil painting that screams expensive, and replace it with something you enjoy looking at. Change procedures from the traditional, staid standards, and open up a new flow for peak performance.

Stop insisting that your wardrobe, your office and your performance be flawless. Stop buying into how others define a successful leader, CEO, entrepreneur or manager. Allow yourself to be true. Minor changes will generate a new, authentic energy in every aspect of your life.

Authenticity is also about allowing others to be who they are. Individuals operate best when they feel appreciated for who they are. Praise the unique contributions of every individual in your pack. Leaders need followers; followers choose to get behind leaders who are aware of, and appreciate, their individual skills. Not everyone can be a

CEO or leader; not everyone needs to be. Someone has to do the accounting; someone has to generate the sales. If individuals don't perform at peak levels throughout your company, the leaders can't get anything done.

Allow each wolf to be who and what it is. Encourage authenticity in your pack. Give everyone the flexibility to enact changes in their own procedures that enhance the work flow. They will actively seek out the why behind their tasks. They will constantly assess whether their efforts are creating the impact they, and you, desire. With meaning and the ability to work as individuals toward that common goal, your entire company will become authentic.

*Action Step:* **Occasionally become the lone wolf.** As a leader, sometimes you'll have to strike out on your own. By going up to the top of that windy ridge, you'll be able to see out across your territory and the territories of others. You'll note any threats closing in and locate the herds that feed your pack.

When you bring this information back to the team, you might find that you're still the lone wolf. Your ideas and opinions might not mesh with the narrow viewpoints others have. Stay strong. Remember that being alone does not mean being lonely. Instead, it means being the one true voice.

If the external pressure creates doubts, take some time to sit quietly with your ideas. Calm your mind, and listen to your heart in silence. Allow information to arise from your subconscious … thoughts, experiences and information will arrive to support your new idea. If not, you'll have gained new wisdom. When you've found that support for your path, bring the conscious mind back online to create the plans and procedures you need to ensure success.

*Action Step:* **Implant the entrepreneurial spirit.** In addition to being aware of and praising your pack's abilities and accomplishments, implement "The Spirit of Entrepreneurial Leadership™" program. Every quarter, ask everyone in your entire company to submit ideas on how to improve the company. Items might run the gambit from dressing up the lobby with a fresh coat of paint to changing the type of ads you run.

While a suggestion box is fine, no one ever really knows if those slips of paper are looked at or if they just disappear into a black hole. By asking every individual for ideas on a scheduled basis, your efforts will be seen as authentic.

Be sure to take action. Select the best suggestion, and assign it to someone right away. If you'd like to double the results, try to assign the task to the individual who made the suggestion. Have them oversee the contractors who repaint the lobby, or ask them how the ads might change.

Your follow-up will go a long way toward inspiring passion and enthusiasm in the whole team. Because you are aware of individuals, they become more aware of themselves. With authentic attention, they grow more authentic in their own respect for their individual talents. Everyone wins!

## PAWS FOR REFLECTION

*Live the Entrepreneurial Spirit every day.*

## CHEAT SHEET

# The Wolf's-Eye View

- Occasionally you must step away from the pack to gain a wider perspective.

- In choosing to have an individual voice and in taking responsibility for our decisions and mistakes, we breathe the breath of freedom.

- The largest variable between your company and your competition is the culture in which your organization operates.

- Old-school thinking has given way to The Spirit of Entrepreneurial Leadership™.

- Spirit is a connection between mind and emotions.

- An entrepreneurial company is self-directed and creative.

- Leadership is the ability to influence and gain commitment from others.

- Reading a book won't make anyone a leader. Incorporate your values and beliefs, your vision and goals, your purpose and passion—in yourself and within your organization.

- People are emotional beings. They are the only resource that can improve the bottom line through passion and enthusiasm.

- Feelings have a place at work. Utilize them for maximum results.

- Purpose and passion work together. People have passion when they understand the purpose of their actions, the answer to the question, "Why?"

## CHEAT SHEET

- Asking "Why?" generates a response. Responses generate knowledge. Knowledge generates more questions.

- Be willing to reward success and intelligent failure. Thinking outside the box won't generate results every time, but without risk, your company will stagnate.

**Free tools at www.HowlLeadership.com**
*(Use VIP Code: ALPHA)*

# The Ultimate Wolf Way

Wolves are bright, adaptable creatures. They don't waste time or energy. During summer, they stake out the meadows where they know deer will come to feed. When the snow piles up in winter, the pack walks in the trail broken by the lead animal to conserve energy. The wolves target the weak and ill among their prey to make the hunt more efficient. When large prey are unavailable, the wolves subsist quite well on smaller game; and lone animals can thrive on a diet of rodents.

Wolves live in the now. They take advantage of every opportunity while defending their territories. Only one pair breeds, yet the entire pack cares for the litter. The pack's hierarchy ensures that everyone knows exactly what's expected and how to act. They communicate constantly and naturally, and they function with their true natures unburdened by baggage. Best of all, they know how to howl.

Wolves are the ultimate leaders of themselves and their environments.

### First-Generation Results

If you're looking for change, the advice will often be to take a long term perspective. Building anything worthwhile takes time, right? Right. But in many cases results can be dramatic within what I call the "first generation".

You want efforts that generate results in their first incarnation, procedures that create success their first time out. You know from other chapters that people won't always succeed and that failure is a part of success. Even wolves don't bring down prey every time. But there are things you can do to achieve fast, powerful results.

On a personal level, it can be as simple as the example of Jim's presentation earlier: if Jim had stopped to reconstruct his automatic thought pattern, he could have delivered a presentation that had his management rearing to get out and start implementing his plans. At a company level, it can be as simple as recognizing that the leaders set the tone for the pack. Once the leaders pay attention to their attitude—literally check it at the door—the change in attitude of individuals will be quickly apparent. The results in terms of productivity will speak for themselves: efficiency, satisfaction and creativity.

As I created my own success, I constantly asked questions and worked up cheat sheets in a similar vein to those included in this book. By using notes that highlighted important points and critical concepts, I could think through problems and processes in detail. Next time a situation came up, I'd refer to the cheat sheet and know exactly what to do. With every new use, I improved the procedures. I kept practicing until they became ingrained.

I also shared them with my staff. My philosophy is, if I can teach you how to do something I've been doing, you learn and grow and can push me up the ladder. And I'll take you with me. All my employees had to have procedures in place. "In case someone gets run over by a Mack truck," I'd say when they asked why. "We'll send flowers, but the job still has to get done." This kind of attitude allowed results to be seen without others needing to "reinvent the wheel". First generation.

For the most part, I was the sole woman among the men who dominated the construction business. Early in my career, I consciously chose where I sat at the conference table and what I wore. When meeting with bankers, I dressed like a banker—in a suit, often black or red power colors, always professional. Then I'd suggest we take the language down to a Dick-and-Jane level.

"You can use your financial terms," I'd say, "and I can talk construction speak, and we'll both walk out wondering what the other meant. Or we can communicate on a common level and get the end result we both want to achieve."

No one floundered in deep snow. We walked the path of everyday efficient and effective language, an easier road that conserved our energy and got us to our destination much more quickly. Because I had adapted my dress to appear like them, they were immediately more comfortable. They didn't have to wonder about the species called "woman in construction" or whether the financial banker species would be able to relate to me. We both came to the table knowing we were feeling beings, humans who were in control and who could choose common ground.

So, as well as ensuring those around you are comfortable enough to focus on the job at hand, keep track of *how* you created your success by noting down what you learn and how you applied those lessons. And once you have those processes right, you're ready to learn a principle that will enable you to plant yourself in a position of strength for the long term.

## Which Wolf Wins?

One evening an old Cherokee told his grandson about a battle that goes on inside people.

"My son," he said, "the battle is between two spirit wolves inside us all. One spirit is evil. It is anger, envy, jealousy, sorrow, regret, greed, arrogance, self-pity, guilt, resentment, inferiority, lies, false pride, superiority and ego. The other spirit is good. It is joy, peace, love, hope, serenity, humility, kindness, benevolence, empathy, generosity, truth, compassion and faith."

After thinking about it for a minute, the grandson asked, "Which wolf wins?"

"The one you feed."

You're going to feed your good wolf with the most powerful tool yet—Strategic E-magination (imagine with emotions). Remember that it's not enough to break old patterns; you must replace them with something new. It's also not enough to throw out old stories that anticipate failure and generate fear; you must replace them with something useful and positive. Strategic E-magination ensures that every step on your path to optimal success is efficient, powerful and effective.

Start at the end. Mentally experience your future achievements while fully engaging all your senses. Remember that the brain can't tell what's real and not real; it sends out the same chemical signals when you visualize something as when you actually experience it in real life. Your body therefore responds as if the imagined event actually happened. With that brain-body team working for you, you automatically act in ways that will achieve your goals.

*Action step:* **Hunt for your prize.** With a tablet and pen at hand, find a comfortable, quiet space where you can be totally alone for at least an hour. If you can be outside, all the better. Turn off the TV, stereo, iPod and phone. *Turn them off!*

Now close your eyes. Take five deep breaths. Breathe in all the way, expanding your chest and belly. Hold it for a count of five. Then let the air out very slowly. Feel your body melt into relaxation. Do this at least five times.

With your eyes still closed, picture the last time you remember feeling truly happy. Where were you? How old were you? What were you doing? Was anyone with you? Was it night or day? Were you inside or out? Was it raining or sunny? Look around and see what colors pop out. Smell the air or the food cooking. Hear the rain pounding or the people laughing. Remember what you touched, the rough and smooth textures. Take it all in.

When you feel every essence of this image throughout your body, slowly open your eyes and begin writing. Write every detail. Don't worry about spelling, grammar or punctuation. Capture the picture. Capture your feelings. Capture your senses. You might find that when you begin to write, you remember more details. That's fine, just keep going. When there is nothing more to write, turn the page. Keep repeating this exercise until you can't bring any more truly happy times to your consciousness.

*Action step:* **Examine your prize.** The written pages describe your pictures of happy times. This is your prize. They are you at your happiest moments. When you examine each one from that thirty-thousand-foot level, without emotion or judgment, what similarities do you find?

Maybe you were always out in nature, or always running, dancing and playing. Maybe you were playing sports or were always part of a team. You might have been exploring and having exciting adventures. Possibly you were always by yourself, just being peaceful and becoming better acquainted with your thoughts or your environment or your task. There are no wrong answers. This is all about you and what makes you happy.

On a separate piece of paper, list the different aspects of the stories that brought you happiness. *I enjoy being by myself in nature; I enjoy fly-fishing; I like long walks by myself.* There's a trend there. *I enjoy white water rafting; I enjoy parasailing; I like riding my motorcycle* . . . yet another trend. *I enjoy family picnics; I enjoy spending time with my friends; I like neighborhood block parties.* You've got it!

Look deeper. What about these different aspects do you truly enjoy? Maybe when you're fly-fishing you feel powerful and alive. When you parasail, you feel exhilarated and out of control. Enjoying a picnic with family and friends means you're part of something . . . you belong. Dig deep and see why these people, places, things or events bring you pleasure.

*Action step:* **Hold onto the prize.** Now that you've identified the specific aspects that make you happy, it's time to ignite the ember! Integrate your passion into your daily routine. Maybe you enjoy travel and you're a great salesperson. Is there a position that will send you out to see the world? If you enjoy being alone outdoors but don't want to upset your family, you might plan a weekend trip for yourself along with a separate get-away with your spouse.

Be creative. Arrange for trade-offs. Create a win-win for everyone. Join a league to play your favorite sport. Sign up at the local craft center to expand your creativity. Use your conscious mind to figure out how to embrace your passion instead of using it to line up all the reasons why you can't. Change your lifestyle to fit your passion in daily, weekly, monthly, quarterly and yearly increments.

Just making the plans and taking the steps to implement passion will make you feel much better. The ember ignites new flames. Taking action benefits you and everybody around you. You will be happier, more relaxed and more focused. It's all about you. You are the  Alpha Leader of your life!

*Action step:* **Generate new prizes.** Here's where Strategic E-magination comes in. Begin to imagine your ideal scenario. This is your ultimate goal, the pinnacle of your success. This is the life you will lead when you are happy all the time—when you have everyone and everything running on a smooth, easy upward track. You don't have to have it all nailed down. Allow room for your imagination to fill in the blanks. Put down your pen, and close your eyes again. Breathe deeply just like before, holding at the end of each inhalation before slowly exhaling.

Now picture yourself at that future pinnacle. See the different things and people that are gathered around you. Don't force it! Remember this is not your linear mind, it's your imagination. Hear their voices and laughter; notice the colors. Touch different things, and feel their textures. Smell the fresh outdoor air, or feel the coolness inside. Create the reality of that moment in your mind.

Now make a special note about how you feel. Allow your brain to send the chemicals associated with your relaxed, happy state out into your body. Feel your muscles relax; allow a smile of true pleasure to touch your lips. Experience your pride for all you've accomplished. When you can truly feel the power of your new emotions sinking into your body, gently open your eyes.

Write it down. Include every detail. Again, you might find that you're adding more details than what you visualized. That's fine; it's your conscious mind kicking in to enhance the process. Keep writing until you have a full picture of your peak experience.

This is your cheat sheet for your own future. Keep it. Refer to it every once in a while. Read it over, clear your mind and then picture the same image over and over. Add to it; adjust the details if you like. Remember, you're in control. And since you're adaptable, your image might also adapt as new information arrives and your life changes.

Go with it. Allow your subconscious mind to generate ever-greater pleasures and your conscious mind to take you to ever-greater heights. Modify your cheat sheet as needed and then store it away. Remember, the fact that you're keeping it around impresses your subconscious. *This is important*, you're telling yourself. *Remember this. Create this.*

And you will.

**The Pathfinder**

Native Americans have long regarded wolves as teachers and pathfinders. They are fiercely loyal to their mates, and they have a strong sense of family while maintaining their individualism. Everything in the pack hierarchy supports each member's unique talents and abilities. Each member contributes to the good of the entire pack.

Authentic leadership is the same. You and your team must be free to be yourselves even while your pack maintains its highly organized framework. You must communicate effectively, always knowing that the slightest gesture or inflection will speak louder than your words. You must find new solutions and chart new courses, while maintaining the stability of your corporate structure.

Finally, you must recognize that the intangible aspects of wolf medicine, the subconscious and emotional dealings of human beings, are as important as the logical, real-world applications generated by the conscious mind. By freeing both your minds to function at their fullest capacities, you will find guidance in your imagination, link your intelligence to your intuition, utilize the best of interpersonal and intrapersonal relationships, outwit your enemies and take advantage of every opportunity in your territory.

Your final action step is about choice. You can choose to perform the exercises in this book or merely implement their wisdom. You choose whether to apply some, all or none of these lessons. You can work with these action steps only in your career or allow them to benefit every area of your life. You choose to become the wolf. You choose to **Howl!**

## PAWS FOR THE FUTURE

*You are the Alpha Leader of your mind.*

*You are the leader of your life.*

**What will YOU hunt today?**

# *Be Connected*

**Visit our websites:**

YourClearEdge.com and HowlLeadership.com

- Join our mailing lists and stay current on our latest resources and opportunities.

- Jump onto our Blog and post your success stories, ideas and comments.

- Sign up for seminars and workshops.

**Personal & Business Acceleration Specialist for Non-Stop Success**

- When you have your ClearEdge you are crystal clear, precise and focused—you have peak mental clarity, greater decisiveness and self-discipline. You are destined for greatness. Cut away your competition and become #1 in your personal and professional life. You can have the lifestyle you deserve!

- To receive more information, Deborah@YourClearEdge.com

**Interested in booking Deborah?**

Deborah offers your company or organization the right mix of learning, laughing and enduring benefits during her programs as she draws from her diverse professional and personal background. Street-smart, dynamic and committed to your success, Deborah delivers real life stories, proven systems and fast results.

Contact her for keynotes, workshops and seminars.

**Strategic E-magination for you or your Alpha Leaders**

Design a plan to accelerate you and your business for non-stop success.

Contact Deborah directly via Deborah@YourClearEdge.com or visit <u>YourClearEdge.com</u> for further information.

# *References*

[1] http://www.brucelipton.com/articles/how-your-beliefs-control-your-biology/ viewed 30 March 2010

# *About the Author*

**From answering phones to owning and running a $20 million business ...**

Considered one of the most dynamic personal and business acceleration specialists around, Deborah Dubree has earned a reputation for training serious achievers worldwide to stop wasting time, energy and money and reach their goals. Her radically straightforward, high-energy style puts her in demand as a captivating coach, consultant and keynote speaker. Bold, clear and practical in her approach, Deborah delights in inspiring clients to build their mental agility, communicate for results and walk like a winner ... as they become #1 in their field of expertise.

Tenacious and gutsy, she gained a unique perspective on business during her climb up the ladder of success from answering the phones as an inexperienced receptionist to owning and running a $20 million commercial construction company, all with only a high school diploma.

Along the way she has experienced lows (serious medical conditions, bankruptcy, divorce, death) but she's persevered through it to create the life and business she envisioned. Deborah draws on her life experiences to make her talks even more powerful and transformational.

In addition, her leadership skills earned her several respected positions including: President of Construction Financial Management Association and International President of the Timberline User Group. Her contribution

*more ...*

to the construction industry was so valued, industry peers nominated her National Woman of the Year in Construction.

Eventually, Deborah stepped away from her CEO position to create ClearEdge. **"The old ways of doing business do not work anymore. Feeling leadership, not soft leadership, cuts away your competition, enhances your effectiveness and boosts your personal and professional  bottom line."**

An adventurer, thrill seeker and international traveler, Deborah plays full-out whether she's diving with the great white sharks off the Isle de Guadalupe, ballooning over the Masai Mara in Africa or driving a six-hundred horsepower race car at speeds of well over a hundred miles per hour.

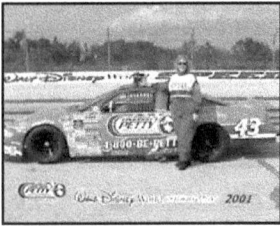

Deborah's greatest achievement and source of joy is being the mother of her two grown children, Kristine and Jason. They live in the Phoenix area along with their loving spouses, Martin and Nicki.

www.ingramcontent.com/pod-product-compliance
Lightning Source LLC
Chambersburg PA
CBHW070348090426
42733CB00009B/1333